WELLNESS REAL ESTATE | MODERN MARKETING FOR REAL ESTATE PROFESSIONALS

LEARN HOW TO LEVERAGE THIS GROWING TREND AND TURN EVERYDAY CONVERSATIONS INTO FOLLOWERS AND LEADS FOR YOUR REAL ESTATE BUSINESS

SHEILA ALSTON

Copyright © 2023 by Sheila Alston

All rights reserved.

No part of this book may be reproduced in any form or by any electronic or mechanical means, including information storage and retrieval systems, without written permission from the author, except for the use of brief quotations in a book review.

❀ Created with Vellum

FOREWORD

Wellness Real Estate: The Fastest Growing Trend That Is Shifting The Industry And Shaping Our Future

Leverage This Momentum to Nurture Your Relationships and Grow Your Business

This book is for real estate agents who want to engage and connect with more people by having more interesting conversations about real estate more often. Learn how you can benefit from this growing demand for healthy living by following the simple strategies in this book. When finished, you'll know how easy it can be to showcase your value, gain more followers and position yourself as a leader in this growing industry segment.

This book is dedicated to all the forward-thinking real estate agents who are merging their passions for healthy living with real estate in order to offer more value to their clients. You are not alone! There is a whole tribe of industry professionals who care about the well-being of their clients and want to help others live healthier, more comfortable, and joyful lives. Inside this book, you'll find a list of professionals doing the same thing. Their contact information is included so you can reach out and network with other like-minded agents.

If you are determined to build a business that not only makes a greater impact but also brings more joy and fulfillment to your life, I wrote this book for you.

INTRODUCTION

Before stepping into the world of real estate, I spent nearly two decades as a stay-at-home mom, watching my children grow up and gradually make their way into adulthood. The thought of my oldest heading off to college left me with a mix of emotions. I had always embraced my role as a mom with enthusiasm, but as my kids started to move on, a nagging question kept me tossing and turning at night: What's next for me? I wasn't *too* worried about the challenges of starting a career in my late 40's. For me, it was more about finding a new purpose, a new direction for this next phase of my life that would also benefit others in some way. Would it be possible to turn a passion into a business? Well yes, I did know that was possible, but could I do it?

If any of you are empty nesters, I'm sure you can relate. The thought of my kids growing up and away was really

INTRODUCTION

sad for while. I had to consciously decide to change my perspective and not let this new phase of my life be filled with sadness and longing for the past. I say this laughing now, but It took several months for me to realize that my life wasn't actually ending. Instead, it could be the beginning of a new chapter, one where I could chase my dreams and learn something new. Little did I know then where this path was leading me.

For most of my life, I've been passionate about healthy living and all things wellness, so when I discovered a year-long program to become a health coach, I was immediately intrigued. After doing some research, I was so excited to enroll. I learned over 140 different food theories and listened to lectures from leading health experts around the world. We also had to practice coaching people and learn how to both manage and market a small business. However, after graduating and receiving my certification, I didn't have the drive to become the health coach like I was anticipating. Something wasn't right, but I couldn't put my finger on precisely what it was.

Over the past 15 years, my husband and I have renovated several houses and moved several times. During this time of reflection, I realized real estate and design were two other passions of mine. In my mind, I knew somehow I needed to bring health & home together, and that search is what led me down the amazing path I'm on now.

INTRODUCTION

Within a few months, I got my real estate license, joined a national brokerage, and started creating a name and brand for myself. If you are an agent, you know how difficult this is! They don't tell you about the long hours it takes to grow a business from scratch or how it can take weeks or even months before you make your first sale. Most agents I know stress about the feast or famine roller coaster of the business. Maybe that's why the majority of agents quit within their first five years.

After doing some online research on health, home, and wellness, I found The Global Wellness Institute. According to them, there was already a Wellness Real Estate industry, and at the time, it was worth $134 Billion worldwide! (As of April 2023, wellness real estate is anticipated to be worth $850B by 2027!![2]) I was so inspired to learn more, and so I started on a fantastic journey that has led me to meet incredible industry professionals marketing themselves differently. This publication summarizes what I've learned so far.

After reading this book:

- You'll better understand what wellness real estate is and how to leverage this growing trend, which will enable you to engage more people about your business and attract more leads.
- You'll find examples of developers, home professionals, and other agents who are infusing

INTRODUCTION

> their passions for healthier living to make a positive impact in the world and stand out among their competitors.
> - And you'll learn simple ways to expand your knowledge and network so you can easily provide more value without having to do more work.

I've intentionally made this book as concise and brief as it can be because I know how busy real estate agents are. I don't want to bog you down with endless details, I'm just so excited to share this fantastic opportunity unfolding right before our eyes. I hope that this book inspires you to be open to the new opportunities all around you. As industry professionals, it is the real estate agent who is in people's homes; agents give advice and refer experts to help their clients with everything related to the home environment. So isn't it logical that real estate agents should also be the ones who learn about this exciting new trend and leverage its momentum to deepen relationships and grow their businesses?

My goal is to give you a brief overview of what is currently happening in the wellness real estate segment as I've seen it unfold with my business through the developers and agents I've had the privilege to interview on my podcasts and the amazing communities I've been able to feature in my magazine, WellnessRE™; I hope that it will trigger new thoughts and ideas that will lead you forward on your path to success and sparks a fire inside you to become the leader and community connector you are meant to be.

Together we CAN make a difference in the world! One home at a time.

CHAPTER 1
WHAT IS WELLNESS REAL ESTATE?

"Man cannot discover new oceans unless he has the courage to lose sight of the shore." - Andre Gide

---

Would it surprise you to learn that your attached garage and private backyard actually serve to reinforce the exact opposite of what is required to lead a healthier lifestyle? How does this style of living encourage social interaction with neighbors? And is that important to our overall sense of well-being? What other elements of our home environment can be improved to support our connection to ourselves and others?

. . .

These types of questions have kept forward-thinking developers thinking for the past 20 years, and as a result, a brand-new segment of the industry has emerged called Wellness Real Estate. While living a healthy lifestyle has always been on trend, until recently, most people did not make the connection between health and home. For too many years, it has been cheaper and easier to live secluded sedentary lives filled with an excess of junk foods and junk media filling our minds. And as more and more people begin realizing there is a connection between lifestyle and health, the demand for products and services that help us achieve a more holistic approach to healthy living will grow.

The nonprofit Global Wellness Institute (GWI) is the leading research organization for the wellness industry. In 2018 they identified 740 wellness residential projects around the world. In 2021 they said the sector has since grown so fast that the projects were too many to count correctly. As of November 2021, the GWI "conservatively estimates that there are over 2,300 wellness projects worldwide (either built, partially built, or in development)."[1] Most recently, in a press release by Technavio,[2] "Wellness real estate market size is to grow by USD 575.9 billion from 2022 to 2027; increasing demand for regenerative living to be an emerging trend."

> "The Global Wellness Institute (GWI) defines wellness real estate as the construction of residential and commercial/institutional properties (including office, hospital, mixed-use/multifamily, medical and leisure) that incorporate intentional wellness elements in their design, materials and building, as well as their amenities, services and/or programming." - GWI[3]

So the idea of living in a community that, from the beginning, was planned to be supportive of health and well-being is truly inspiring. This isn't just a marketing ploy where the developer simply added a fitness center and gets to call it a wellness neighborhood. No, these are communities where every decision was made to create a place where residents can thrive. The great news is that when people help people, they are rewarded. So even though profit isn't the main objective in the design, these new communities are blazing a trail where demand has followed; people in these neighborhoods are happier and healthier, and as such, property values are also higher.

After all, who doesn't like the idea of having direct access to fresh organic food, nature beckoning right outside your door, and the ability to walk along edible trails to meet friends at a local coffee shop or farmers market to grab a bite to eat? If you're wondering, what's the catch? There isn't one. In the last chapter, I list out all the communities that I'm currently aware of that are bringing new ways of experiencing joyful living to families. No two communities are exactly alike, and they bring with them a whole list of incredible healthy amenities that lucky residents get to enjoy on a daily basis.

Through my research, I have found 5 different types of wellness lifestyle communities:

1. Agrihoods
2. Naturehoods
3. Leisurehoods
4. Urban Wellness Communities
5. Minimalist or Tiny Living

Agrihood

Agirhoods are neighborhoods that center around a farming component. They emphasize farm-to-table living and usually provide education and access to an organic and sometimes regenerative farm. Agrihoods allow residents to interact with the farmers, essentially growing and eating organic whole foods right from their own backyard.

Nothing gets fresher than that! More and more people feel commercial agriculture is slowly killing us with pesticides and other toxins, and they are seeking ways to have more control of what goes in their bodies. So Agrihoods are making farm-to-table living an accessible alternative to traditional housing. The farm component provides the perfect centerpiece for the neighborhood that promotes social connection and interaction through a neighborhood farmers market, which makes it easy for people to meet and make new friends. Although each Agrihood is unique, sustainability, healthy eating, community, and belonging are always integral to the overall design and development of the community.

Naturehood

Naturehoods are communities that offer residents more direct access to nature but don't necessarily center around an organic farm. Whether it be hiking or biking trails, or neighborhood dog parks, community members of Naturehoods are able to enjoy more of the great outdoors. Many of these Naturehoods also consider themselves to be Surban communities. Surban is a term that combines the best of urban and suburban living. It is still a very new idea, but these types of communities are highly desirable because they offer suburban features, like more space, with the convenience of easy access to urban amenities, like walkability to dining and shopping.

. . .

Surban living is expected to grow over the next ten years. According to REonomy[4], at least 80% of millennials and households with young families are anticipated to want this type of living. They are designed for people who want to be more active, making walking, bicycling, and use of local transportation an easy alternative to cars.

Leisurehood

Long before wellness lifestyle communities were even defined, luxurious resort and spa destinations were the ultimate dream for a relaxing vacation destination. Many of these destinations have had real estate that is available on the resort property. This means that access to nature, activities and good healthy food will abound. These neighborhoods will also typically have spas and fitness facilities built in as well. Talk about living like you are on vacation! These leisurehoods are designed with that concept in mind so residents can relax and enjoy life to the fullest. As more and more people are now working from home and able to live anywhere connected to the internet, resort destinations are giving residents the ultimate life of pleasure with world-class service and amenities right out their own front door. As demand for remote-based work has increased, new communities that prioritize the residents over the resort are changing the way living your best life could potentially mean for those who get to call this type of community home.

· · ·

Urban Wellness Communities

Wellness living is not just for families in the burbs! For those who love to be able to walk or bike to neighborhood restaurants, parks, or to work, an urban city has always been the choice over suburbia. Today, city dwellers can experience an elevated level of well-being as metropolitan areas across America have more and more healthy dining options, different types of workout and exercise facilities to choose from, and access to alternative medical treatments not usually as available in suburban areas.

Some people just love being connected to the energy of fast pace living and forward-thinking developers are tapping into being able to design urban residential communities that offer more than covered parking and a weight room.

Minimalist or Tiny Living

Another type of housing that has been exploding in recent years appeals to minimalists. To these folks, well-being means living by the concept of "less is more" which gives them more freedom to travel and experience the world rather than to spend all their time working just to accumulate more things like a bigger house, more furniture, and cars.

. . .

According to industry reports,[6] "One-fourth of U.S. Millennials expect to always rent" because as home prices continue to increase, they have given up on the idea that homeownership could be a realistic possibility. New companies like ORI which provide have made small spaces larger by the use of their robotic moveable furniture allowing small spaces to have multiple functions. Inspired by origami, ORI is taking minimalist living to new heights. Learn more at: https://www.oriliving.com/

A home that is under 600 sqft is generally considered a tiny home however, the typical tiny house is around 225 sqft. Not all minimalists choose to live in a tiny home, but all tiny homeowners will be minimalists. Across the country, you can now find tiny homes on wheels allowing homeowners to move locations to what are called pop-up neighbors. These areas can serve as both permanent residences or a destination for visitors. Tiny living gives people the option of leading simpler lives with low expenses and lots of freedom. From eco-villages to vacation retreats, tiny home communities are not like the mobile home parks of the past, these homes typically have lots of design savvy and are charming to the eye. Those that live the tiny life are a close-knit community because they all desire to live simpler lives, and are interested in sustainability.

. . .

What about senior living?

The reason I didn't categorize senior living into a wellness lifestyle community is that the current trend is moving back towards multi-generational living as it once was many years ago. Seniors who lose touch with their families and who don't have a purpose in their lives deteriorate faster than those who feel like they are still contributing to their families or to a larger community. While this style of living may have started out of financial necessity, the truth is that most families who support one another by living together in the home or community are less lonely, have a deeper connection to their loved ones, and have a higher sense of happiness. Realtor magazine states[7] that 20% of the population is living under the same roof, and the multi-generational living trend in America is only starting to grow. As more and more seniors prefer to age in place rather than move into an assisted living facility and younger generations want to care for their aging parents, homes that have flexible floorplans that enable adult family members to have more privacy while living together are in high demand.

HOW DOES THIS NEW TREND AFFECT ME AS A REAL ESTATE PROFESSIONAL?

As a real estate professional, you might be wondering, "Why should I care about this new trend in development? I sell existing homes."

While demand for a new home or community that is supportive of a healthy lifestyle continues to grow and is shaping how homes will be built in the future, the fact is, that according to the National Association of REALTORS®[7], as much as 88% of homes sold are *existing homes*, not new homes.

If this was one of the thoughts that crossed your mind, then you are onto something since this is *exactly* where the big opportunity lies.

Because EVERYONE deserves to live in a healthy home, not just the people who can afford to buy one in a new wellness lifestyle community.

So if *everyone* deserves to live in a healthy home, how *is everyone* going to learn what it means to have a healthy home? How are they going to know what upgrades are good choices for health *and* resale? How are they going to know who is the best carpet supplier for non-toxic carpet options when they remodel? These are just a few of the questions that I want you to ponder as you read through this book.

If development is trending towards wellness, and no one else is talking about this, shouldn't I start educating my audience about these topics?

My thoughts exactly….

CHAPTER 2
WHAT IS A HEALTHY HOME

"The objective of cleaning is not just to clean, but to feel happiness living within that environment." - Marie Kondo

Wellness in real estate is a broad umbrella that, in my mind, encompasses healthy, green and sustainable homes. You might be wondering, so what exactly is a healthy home anyway? Is it the same as a green or energy-efficient home? Or a sustainable home? In this chapter, you'll learn the differences between the terminology and what the intention is behind each one. We won't spend a long time here, but it's important for you to understand the basics if you want to talk confidently about this subject with your followers.

. . .

In chapter 6, I have compiled a list of wellness lifestyle communities nationwide. Many of these communities have different levels of green, sustainable, and health-focused features and amenities built into the neighborhood design. So, by reading this chapter and becoming aware of the slight differences in terminology, you'll be better equipped to help educate your clients should they start asking you. Ultimately, it's up to your client to decide which elements are most important to them, so providing this information guides them to make better-informed decisions when buying, selling, and or remodeling.

Sometimes you will hear people use healthy, green, sustainable, or eco interchangeably; however, each term has its own unique definition and intentions, so in practice, they do not always mean the same thing. It's important to understand the mindset or intention behind the words when speaking about this with your clients. There may be opportunities where a choice achieves all three intentions, however, sometimes, they do not. So what are the main differences? I'll go over now, and then we'll dive deeper into each one separately.

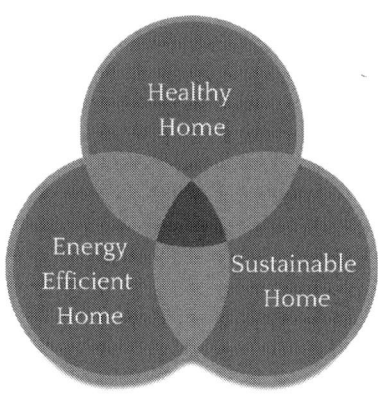

Healthy Home

Intention: To create an environment that is less toxic, feels comfortable and is supportive of the health of the inhabitants.

Green or Energy-Efficient Home

Intention: To lower energy consumption and increase performance and convenience.

Sustainable or Eco Home

Intention: To consume equal to or less than our own resources provide. So getting to Net zero energy, off-grid living, homesteading, recycling, and reuse of materials is essential to this mindset.

. . .

For example, if a client says that they are searching for a green home but then also confides that their child is sensitive to EMF exposure and having a home free of toxins is also important to them, then you might want to put them in touch with a healthy home expert rather than simply a green home expert. The reason for this is that high-performance homes utilize a lot of smart home wifi technology, and if someone is sensitive to EMF radiation, a 100% true green home may not be the best decision for them. This doesn't mean that this family can't have any high-performing features in their home, it just means that the professional you connect them with should understand all the elements that go into a "healthy home" as well. As an agent, you can connect them with the right professional who is going to help them make better-informed decisions for their family. We'll dive more into this in chapter 6 when we discuss what it means to be a wellness-focused real estate professional.

A DEEPER DIVE INTO HEALTHY HOMES

Remember, the intention of a healthy home is to create an environment that is less toxic, feels comfortable and supports the health of the inhabitants.

When I first started researching this topic a few years ago, there wasn't much information regarding healthy homes beyond air and water quality. Yet I could find tons of separate information from what I call healthy home professionals like Feng Shui practitioners, Color Psychologists, Biophilic and Eco Designers just to name a few. So I decided to combine what I've learned and create my own list of what goes into a healthy home.

There are seven elements of a healthy home, five are essential, and the last two are optional:

1. It's calm
2. It's clean & well-maintained
3. It's dry & well-ventilated
4. It's safe
5. It's less toxic
6. It can also have energy-efficient and sustainable features
7. It can also have wellness amenities added in

1. A Healthy Home is Calm

Having a healthy environment in which you live can help you feel better and more at peace, which helps prevent negative thoughts from creeping in on you. Creating a calm atmosphere in your home gives you a clearer mind and better overall judgment, influencing how you think and act.

· · ·

When you feel relaxed and renewed, you are distracted from everyday problems and stress triggers, which makes your mind feel at ease. This is essential for your body's ability to renew itself. I like to imagine that just like my cell phone tells me how much battery life it has left, our bodies inform us when we are depleted through symptoms of fatigue, overwhelm, and irritability. Giving your body conscious moments of restful relaxation and restorative sleep is essential to getting "full power" back and extending your own "battery" life. There are many ways to create a calm home environment; here are some great ways to get you and your clients started:

- Declutter, because this frees up space in our home and our minds so we can feel less overwhelmed.
- Decorate with calming colors on walls, furniture, art, and accessories.
- Learn more about biophilic design and bring plants into the home.
- Use natural materials.
- Maximize natural light.
- Bring in elements of sound and scents into the house. (think waterfall, essential oils)
- Learn more about Feng Shui principles to create balance and harmony in the space.
- Check out circadian lighting which uses light temperature to mimic the sun, so it naturally

supports our circadian rhythms helping us sleep and wake more peacefully.

2. A healthy home is clean and well-maintained

As a real estate professional, you know the difference between having to sell a messy one vs. one that is tidy and well-maintained. Since I don't want to preach to the choir in this chapter, I'll keep this section brief.

The most obvious reason for keeping a clean home is that allowing dirt, grime, and mess to build up in your home is unsanitary and poses health risks for you and your family. According to a 2013 Household Germ Study[8] by the National Sanitary Foundation, the number of bacteria and viruses on common kitchen appliances and tools may have you reconsidering your cleaning routine.

Statistics[9] from the Centers for Disease Control and Prevention (CDC) estimates that due to food-borne diseases, 48 million people (or 1 in 6 Americans) fall ill; 128,000 end up in the hospital, and 3,000 die.

Here are three things you can do to ensure your home hygiene is healthy[9]:

- Regularly clean your fridge and arrange raw meats away from other foods so spilled juices don't contaminate anything else you are storing. Chicken and ground beef are the most common offenders of causing illness, so place them on a plate or at the bottom of the fridge.
- Lower the toilet lid before you flush because flushing causes bacteria to disperse into the air. Simply putting the lid down before you flush, you minimize germs floating in the air. Also, keeping your toothbrush and hand towels as far away as possible from the toilet helps you spread fewer germs.
- Remove shoes before entering the home. Shoes can bring harmful germs and chemicals such as pollen, pesticides, and salmonella in bird droppings. A University of Arizona study showed that as many as nine different pathogens can survive on shoes[9]. By leaving shoes at the front door, it's less likely these pathogens will be carried into your home.

The second reason to keep a clean, tidy, and well-maintained home is that it frees up mental space and allows you to feel more relaxed at home. Dirty buildup causes you to feel overwhelmed, and if your home environment stays in that chaotic place for too long, it can feel like life is out of control. The more you stay in that emotional state, the more you can start feeling bad about yourself, and life can quickly become quite miserable if this emotional state becomes a regular cycle. On the other hand, having a clean and tidy home gives you a sense of accomplishment. It frees up space in your home and your mind so you can think clearly and be more creative.

Proper maintenance of the home is essential to keeping it healthy as well. Keeping regular tabs on maintenance items ensures that you don't have bigger issues down the road that trigger health issues or become costly to fix later on.

Ten simple things your clients can do to help them keep their home well-maintained: (Feel free to cut and paste this into a flyer for your clients!)

(Consider turning this into a pdf that you put on your website as a free download)

1. **Clean The Gutters Twice a Year**
Cleaning your gutters in the spring and fall ensures that your gutters work properly and so water can properly drain away from your home. Neglecting your gutters can lead to costly water leaks, damage, and mold, so it's essential to do to maintain the health and integrity of your home.

2. Inspect The Roof
Cleaning the gutters gives you the perfect opportunity to inspect the roof and allows you to look for missing, cracked, or damaged shingles that could allow in moisture.

3. Keep Shrubs and Trees Away From The House
Shrubs and trees growing around your house might offer shade that helps keep your home cool in the summer, but when they get too close, they can cause damage to your home. Trees that grow too close to the house provide easy access for squirrels and other animals to find shelter in your attic. When bushes grow too close to your siding, it can allow pests and water damage to your home's structure. Trim shrubs and trees away from the house and the outdoor A/C unit.

4. Check For Drafty Windows And Doors
Feel for leaks in windows and around and underneath exterior doors to ensure you aren't wasting energy heating or cooling the outside. Caulking windows and replacing damaged or missing weatherstrips around exterior doors will save you money on your heating and cooling bills.

5. Fix Leaky Faucets
Fixing a leaky faucet is typically a simple matter of

replacing the rubber washer inside the faucet handle, so it's a great DIY fix.

6. Don't Flush Money Down The Toilet

Leaking toilets can be costly by spiking up your water bill. To determine whether or not you have a leak, put some food coloring in the tank and come back in an hour to see if the color is leaching out into the bowl. If water is leaking from the tank to the bowl, you should replace the rubber flapper inside the tank. If the toilet is leaking around the base, the toilet will need to be replaced.

7. Inspect Washer/Dryer - Hoses And Lint Trap

Washing machines are a leading cause of water damage, and these leaks typically come from the supply and drain hoses, not the machines themselves. Replace the hoses immediately if you see any signs of leaking, damage, or rust around the metal ends of the lines. Replacing them every three years is a good preventative measure. Be sure to remove lint from your dryer's lint trap after every use because the material left inside presents a serious fire hazard.

8. Check Your Refrigerator Door Seals

The seals around your refrigerator doors keep the inside of your refrigerator cold. If they fail, your refrigerator will be less efficient, which can even shorten its lifespan. In order to test the door seals, all you need is a piece of paper. Close your refrigerator door on a piece of paper, and if you can't pull it out of the closed door, then your seals are fine. If not, you need to replace your refrigerator door seals; new ones can be found at any home improvement store.

9. Vacuum Your Refrigerator Condenser Coils

Vacuuming the dust off the condenser coils that are located on the back of the refrigerator extends its life and keeps it running more efficiently. This only needs to be done once a year to be helpful.

10. Replace Your HVAC Filter

Replace HVAC filters a minimum of every six months or every 30 to 90 days if someone in your home has allergies or asthma or if you have pets. Doing this regularly reduces strain on your HVAC system and keeps your indoor air clean and healthy.

There are several different types of air filters to choose from, and they will each have a MERV or Minimum Efficiency Reporting Value. Residential grade air filters are typically a MERV 8. However, HEPA (High-Efficiency Particulate Air) filters range from MERV 16-20. The higher the MERV value, the greater its ability to remove smaller airborne contaminants. However, simply selecting the highest MERV rating may not necessarily be a good choice for your HVAC system as it will cause the system to have to push harder to get air through the filter, which can cause issues if your system is very old or wasn't designed to handle high MERV filters. So it's best to check with the manufacturer of your system or to call your local HVAC technician to ensure you find the right filter that meets your needs. This can get confusing pretty quickly for many consumers, so having a preferred HVAC technician you trust to refer to your clients is an invaluable service you are providing them!

3. A Healthy Home is dry and well-ventilated:

As an industry professional, you already know that trapped moisture is one of the leading causes of mold and mildew growth, so ensuring a home is dry is essential to a healthy home environment. But as new homes and more energy-building practices are being utilized, the building envelope has become more and more airtight, which means toxins can be trapped inside the home. So proper ventilation and bringing fresh air into the home while moving toxic air out is also a vital component of good Indoor Air Quality or IAQ.

There is a bit of a balancing act that is required between dry and moist air because while we want the home to be dry, the air shouldn't be too dry or it can cause itchy skin, eyes, and nasal passages making you more susceptible to colds. While every home is different, humidity levels between 30 and 40 percent are usually ideal for keeping your home warm and comfortable during winter months without leaving condensation on the windows. In the summer, that level is between 50 and 60 percent. There are humidity-measuring devices that can be found online.

4. A Healthy Home is Safe:

Modern homes in the United States are built to code which means that they are regulated and have safety standards that are designed to keep us healthy and safe. So things like railings on stairs, the height of steps, the number of light fixtures on the exterior of a home, and electrical requirements are just a few examples of things that are mandated in codes set by the state and local government building authorities. In order to build a new home, developers and building contractors will need to apply for permits and have inspections done to ensure they adhere to current building codes.

It's a good idea for real estate agents to meet the local builders in your area. Find out more about the type of building they do and see if you can find green or healthy builders you can learn from and build relationships with. Surprise them with your questions about a healthy home and see what they say!

5. A Healthy Home is Less Toxic:

Knowing that it would be near impossible to remove all the toxins in your environment, we'll have to settle on "a little less toxic" which is better than more toxic. Anything you can do to lighten the toxic load on your body will give back to your immune system because you are taxing it less. So understanding what toxins to be aware of is an important aspect, as well as knowing what safe alternatives you have will empower you to make healthier buying decisions.

There are many books and websites that go deep into the toxic home environment, however, as a real estate professional, it's not your job to be the expert on every subject. Surround yourself with home health experts you can refer your clients to. The more you network and learn from these people, the more you will be able to answer simple questions and demonstrate knowledge, but then you'll be able to hand it off. Continue to support your clients by being their connection to trusted healthy home professionals in your area.

6. A Healthy Home also strives to be more Sustainable and Energy Efficient:

In this chapter, I've emphasized the distinctions between a Green or Energy-Efficient Home, a Sustainable Home, and a Healthy Home. Although it's possible for a healthy home to incorporate elements from all three categories, there will be instances where homeowners must prioritize one aspect over the others based on their family's needs.

It's crucial to recognize that people might prioritize different aspects depending on their budget and specific health conditions. Just like in nutrition, achieving a healthier home can be approached in various ways. While we strive to set a good example by leading a "green" lifestyle, it's essential not to judge others for their choices. Everyone's situation is unique, and their decisions may not always align with the most sustainable or energy-efficient options available.

Let me give you a couple of examples:

1. A client wants to buy a home with an induction range in the kitchen. It's the latest and greatest energy-efficient model, and since the home is on solar, it allows the home to be sustainable and reduces energy consumption. A gas range is believed to be more toxic, so this should be a great feature that everyone should be excited about, right? Not necessarily. An induction range uses magnets to create heat, and when you touch the pan to cook something, you are now part of that electromagnetic field. For someone who has any chronic illness or disease, this may be a

terrible health option for them. Instead, choosing and electric range that is not induction or a high-end gas range that has sealed burners and educating them to be sure to use the ventilation and open windows when cooking may be a healthier choice for that family. And so again, it will be important to connect these individuals with a healthy home expert who can guide them.

2. A client who is doing a home remodel wants to buy carpet for the entire home, and they have just come across recycled nylon carpet that is completely sustainable and affordable. But you know their toddler has allergies, and your client has also complained about migraine headaches. Even though recycled nylon is a sustainable choice, it is not a healthy choice. Nylon carpet is a synthetic that is similar to plastic, during the manufacturing process, it is sprayed with all sorts of toxic chemicals to keep it flame-resistant, and stain resistant, then they typically use binders and adhesives that are made with formaldehyde which is a known carcinogen. These chemicals continue to off-gas in the home for five years or more. Knowing a young child might be playing on the floor often, this is not a healthy choice and if someone in the home has lower immune function, it would not be a healthy choice for that family. Instead, send them to check out some healthier choices and let them make a more informed decision. Here are some great resources to refer

them to: Earthweave, Hook & Loom, Organic Weave, Rugs by Roo, and Willaby

It's likely that a homeowner will want to strive to achieve all three elements in a home, so it is healthy, green, and sustainable. However, as their agent and guide, you can provide enormous value to them by helping them understand the differences so they can talk to healthy home experts and make better-informed choices that will work best for them.

7. Wellness features and amenities:

A healthy home can also have features and amenities that enhance and promote a healthy lifestyle. Here are some examples of wellness features that people love. Most agents will market these features on a listing, but how often do you find that they make the connection between health and home?

Finding ways to showcase these features as supportive of the health and vitality that everyone wants is a way you can shine as a listing agent. When homeowners see that you understand the benefits that these upgrades offer to prospective homebuyers (rather than simply stating that it's there), helps them see the value that you provide.

. . .

Here are some wellness features trending in residential homes today:

- Home gym or fitness room
- Meditation space
- Creativity space or homeschool classroom
- Mud room with hand-washing station and shoe storage to keep toxins out
- Indoor/outdoor living areas
- Kitchens that have room for 2+ cooks for more social interaction
- Dual home offices
- Sport Courts
- Putting greens
- Outdoor kids playground
- Pool or plunge pool
- Spa/ Hot Tub
- Jacuzzi tub
- Steam shower
- Infrared Sauna or in-home sauna
- A vegetable garden or fruit trees
- Skylights
- Whole house water filtration system
- HRV or ERV - ventilation system
- Air purification systems - This is the one I recommend; it doesn't use filters and instead uses advanced surface and air purification technology. www.vollara.com. This link takes you to Monica Kahio's site; she has been on my podcast and

helps people with home air, water, and laundry systems.
- Laundry Pure 2.0 - you must check this out (it hooks up to the back of the washing machine and uses air purification technology to clean the water, so you don't need detergent, and it cleans the clothes and the machine! No more smelly washer from the mildew that is stuck inside!) I just got one from Monica myself, and it's amazing!

A DEEPER DIVE INTO GREEN OR ENERGY-EFFICIENT HOMES

Intention: To lower energy consumption and increase performance and convenience.

Sometimes I hear agents say that green homes have been around forever and "most people just don't care about being green." This is one of the biggest myths about green homes. Maybe it's because, for a long time, the idea of being "green" meant that you were a hippie who wanted to go live off the grid somewhere with a grass roof. Many people also think being green is just about recycling, having solar, or being energy efficient. Some even think having green features in a home is cost-prohibitive. In any case, times have changed, and what most consumers think today has shifted.

. . .

The truth is that we are doing so many GREEN things everyday. The sale of cars using electrical or alternative energy sources has risen 81% from 2017 to 2018. As of Dec 2020, more than 1.3 million electric vehicles were on the road, a number that was almost non-existent in 2010. But here's an interesting statistic:

According to the National Resource Defense Council[10], Residential energy efficiency is the largest potential source of CO_2 reduction— even more than making every car electric!

That means there is a huge opportunity and potential for us as agents to be the guide that helps clients make decisions that are good for them, their wallets, AND the planet!

The good news is that consumer demand for savings and being environmentally friendly is rising. The younger generation cares about paying things forward and being kind and authentic to each other and the planet.

Government policy is also shifting in some states as they try to be more proactive on these issues. California is one of the highest solar-generating states in the nation. Over 4,885,000 homes had solar in 2017[11]. New government mandates in 2020 California was the first state to dictate that every new home must have solar. The impact of this is that it will be an expected feature in existing homes very soon. California also passed laws so we can only buy energy-efficient lightbulbs, so now we all do this. We recycle, use programmable thermostats, and try to reduce water consumption when we can. These are just a few things we already do, but there is so much more! And it's only a matter of time before other states begin to follow suit. As consumer demand increases and state mandates shift, you can see the tide moving toward wellness. I wonder what is happening in your state?

As real estate professionals, it's our job to educate our clients and guide them to a home that fits their needs. It's also an excellent opportunity to show them your expertise by being able to guide them to government rebates or connecting them with other green home or healthy home experts that can help them.

There are many more green products that provide better efficiency and save us money on the market today than there were just 10 years ago. There are also many tools available that help us rate how much energy we consume. The good news is that all of this awareness around lowering our energy consumption has provided us with many new alternatives. Here are some companies that provide green building standards and certifications to homes and businesses:

- The Environmental Protection Agency (EPA) has green building standards[12].

- **LEED** (Leadership in Energy and Environmental Design), issued by U.S. Green Buildings Council, is easily the most recognized sustainable and energy-efficient building certification available. There are nine separate certification programs, including ones for commercial, retail, new construction, existing buildings, and more. Every program has a points-based rating system for each green building feature, and the point total determines whether you're LEED Certified, LEED Silver, LEED Gold, or LEED Platinum (the highest level).

- Another well-known green building certification that's offered through the Department of Energy and the Environmental Protection Agency is **Energy Star**. In order to qualify, your building needs to be at least 15% more energy efficient than traditional properties and these certifications will last for one year.

- **BREEAM** (the Building Research Establishment Environmental Assessment Method) is an international program recognizing sustainable buildings and infrastructure projects. A star rating from one to six and a designation of "pass," "good," "very good," "excellent," or "outstanding" comes with the certification. BREEAM-certifications are available on new construction, in-use, or refurbishment projects.

- The Green Globes certification program is offered through **the Green Building Initiative** and consists of three categories which are new construction, existing buildings, and interiors. In order to qualify, at least 35% of the program's 1,000 available points must be met. The process starts with an online survey, then a third-party on-site assessment, and then there is also a post-assessment.

- The **Living Building Challenge** certification factors your building's sustainability performance over 12 months. To qualify, all seven "petals," which include materials, site, water, health, equity, beauty, and energy need to be achieved.

- The **National Association of Home Builders**, the NGBS designation provides a sustainable home certification for residential properties only (including single-family homes, multi-family properties, and mixed-use developments.) Similar to LEED, it has different levels of certification, ranging from Bronze to the highest level, which is Emerald.

- The **GreenGuard** certification is about air quality. This certification focuses on low-emission building materials, mold prevention, moisture protection, and more. There are various planning meetings, reviews, test groups, and compliance testing required before a final certification is awarded.

- **Fitwell** is a certification for new and existing buildings that includes designing spaces for health and productivity. They have a double-blind certification process where two independent reviewers assess each project and then confirm a numerical score. Because Fitwell was developed by public health professionals, this method ensures each review is unbiased and consistent to earn 1, 2, or 3 stars.

- Awarded by the International WELL Building Institute, **The WELL Building Standard** measures sustainability using seven core concepts, including air, water, nourishment, light, movement, and more. This certification focuses on the overall impact of buildings on human health and well-being

---

A DEEPER DIVE INTO SUSTAINABLE OR ECO HOMES

Intention: To consume equal to or less than our own resources provide. So getting to Net zero energy, off-grid living, homesteading, recycling, and reuse of materials is essential to this mindset.

· · ·

While the term Green Home is often used interchangeably with Sustainable Home, there is a slight difference. A home with green features may have improved energy efficiency, but it may not be low enough to qualify as a truly sustainable property. Sustainability is a much more encompassing term, since it considers how the home exists today, but also how it affects the future well-being of both the environment and the inhabitants of the home.

According to Google: "A sustainable home is **one that is built or retrofitted in a way that conserves resources, optimizes energy and water use and that will last longer with quality systems**. A sustainable house is built with low-impact, high-performance materials. They are efficient in terms of manufacturing, shipping, and installing."

NEW CONSTRUCTION TIPS FOR BUILDING A SUSTAINABLE HOME

Discover essential tips for constructing an eco-friendly home that stands the test of time. These insights will help you minimize waste, enhance durability, and boost energy and water efficiency throughout your home's lifespan. By integrating sustainable features from the beginning, you'll reap long-term benefits for both your wallet and the environment.

. . .

INTEGRATE PASSIVE SOLAR DESIGN

Passive solar design is a sustainable building technique that utilizes the sun's energy to heat and cool a home without the need for mechanical or electrical devices. It takes advantage of the natural heat and light from the sun to create a comfortable indoor environment.

Key elements of passive solar design include:

Orientation: Positioning the building in a way that maximizes exposure to the sun. In the northern hemisphere, this means orienting the longest sides of the house (usually the front and back) towards the south.

Windows and Glazing: Installing windows, skylights, and other transparent materials on the south-facing side of the building to allow sunlight to enter and heat the interior. Proper shading is also essential to prevent overheating in the summer.

Thermal Mass: Incorporating materials with high heat-absorbing capacity (such as concrete, brick, or stone) inside the building. These materials absorb and store heat during the day and release it slowly at night, helping to regulate indoor temperatures.

Insulation: Ensuring the building is well-insulated to retain the heat generated during the day and prevent heat loss at night.

Ventilation: Designing the home to allow natural airflow for cooling in warmer months. This can be achieved through strategically placed windows, vents, and the use of thermal chimneys.

By harnessing the sun's energy through these design principles, passive solar homes can significantly reduce heating and cooling costs, decrease reliance on artificial heating and cooling systems, and minimize the overall environmental impact of the building.

INSTALL HIGH-PERFORMANCE WINDOWS

High-performance windows are essential in sustainable homes because they minimize heat transfer, ensuring energy efficiency. These windows have advanced coatings and insulation, reducing energy loss. By controlling indoor temperatures, they lower heating and cooling needs, leading to significant energy savings and environmental impact reduction. Additionally, they enhance natural light, reducing the need for artificial lighting and further contributing to sustainability efforts.

INVEST IN ENERGY-EFFICIENT APPLIANCES

Investing in energy-efficient appliances is a no-brainer for a more sustainable home. These appliances consume significantly less energy than their standard counterparts, resulting in lower utility bills and reducing the carbon footprint of the household. Additionally, they often have advanced features such as programmable settings and smart technology that enable users to optimize energy usage. Not only does this save money in the long run, but it also aligns with eco-conscious living by conserving resources and decreasing greenhouse gas emissions, making it a win-win for both homeowners and the environment.

UTILIZE A DRIP IRRIGATION SYSTEM

Drip irrigation is a highly efficient watering system that conserves water and is a game-changer for sustainable landscaping. Unlike traditional spray nozzles, which can lead to significant water wastage due to overspray and evaporation, drip irrigation delivers water directly to the plant's root zone. This targeted approach minimizes water loss, ensures plants receive the right amount of moisture, and reduces the overall water usage for landscaping. By adopting drip irrigation, homeowners can make a substantial contribution to water conservation efforts while maintaining lush gardens and landscapes.

USE ECO PAINT

Eco-paints, also known as environmentally friendly or low-VOC (Volatile Organic Compounds) paints, have gained popularity as a more sustainable and health-conscious choice. These paints contain lower levels of harmful chemicals, such as VOCs, which can emit toxic fumes into the air. While they are primarily chosen for their health benefits, modern eco-paints have also made substantial advancements in durability and performance. Paint technology has evolved to offer eco-friendly options that are on par with, or even surpass, the durability of traditional high-VOC paints.

These paints contribute to sustainability in several ways:

Reduced Air Pollution: By containing fewer harmful chemicals, eco-paints improve indoor air quality and decrease harmful emissions into the environment, making them a sustainable choice for both human and ecological well-being.

Conservation of Resources: Some eco-paints use recycled or sustainable materials, and their production is designed to minimize environmental impact, aligning with sustainable practices.

Long-Term Impact: Eco-paints contribute to long-term sustainability by promoting a healthier living environment, reducing the need for repainting due to discoloration or damage, and minimizing the disposal of paint containers and waste.

The great thing is that eco-paints offer the dual benefit of being both a healthier and a more sustainable choice. They not only reduce exposure to harmful chemicals but also minimize their impact on the environment. As paint technology continues to advance, there are now more options than ever for paints that are lower in toxins and kinder to our health and the planet.

CONSIDER A COOL ROOF DESIGN

A cool roof is a roofing system designed to reflect more sunlight and absorb less heat than standard roofs. These roofs are typically made of highly reflective materials or have a reflective coating applied. The primary purpose of a cool roof is to maintain a lower surface temperature, even on hot days, by reflecting a larger percentage of sunlight and emitting absorbed solar radiation.

Cool roofs are beneficial for several reasons:

Energy Efficiency: By reflecting more sunlight and absorbing less heat, cool roofs help reduce indoor cooling needs, leading to lower energy bills and decreased demand for air conditioning.

Urban Heat Island Mitigation: Cool roofs contribute to mitigating the urban heat island effect, where urban areas experience higher temperatures due to human activities and heat-absorbing surfaces.

Extended Roof Lifespan: By reducing the roof temperature, cool roofs may experience less thermal expansion and contraction, potentially leading to a longer lifespan for the roofing material.

Environmental Impact: By lowering energy consumption, cool roofs decrease greenhouse gas emissions, contributing to environmental conservation efforts.

Having a cool roof isn't just about aesthetics; it's about superior performance. A cool roof not only looks good but also functions exceptionally well by reflecting sunlight and reducing heat absorption. This enhanced performance leads to energy savings, a longer roof lifespan, and a more comfortable interior environment. So, when you invest in a cool roof, you're not just making a style statement – you're making a smart, practical choice for energy efficiency and sustainability.

Sustainability is not just about being energy-efficient, but it's also about being efficient overall, which means sourcing local laborers and local products as much as possible rather than importing them from all over the globe. Having the intention to use less or to build in infrastructure that produces as much as you use is a viable way we can make better use of resources to ensure they are there for future generations to enjoy.

AGENT BENEFITS

Connecting with sustainability experts and embracing eco-friendly practices in your real estate business isn't just a smart move – it's a game-changer. As a REALTOR®, you benefit immensely from this knowledge. It positions you as a trusted expert, showing clients that you prioritize their well-being and the environment. Plus, in today's market, more clients are actively seeking green homes, making your expertise in this area incredibly valuable.

I encourage you to connect with sustainability experts in your area, jump into local green building events, join eco-focused associations, and network with architects and builders specializing in green projects. Engaging with energy efficiency programs and exploring online platforms dedicated to sustainability can also expand your network.

By building these connections and incorporating eco-friendly advice into your real estate marketing materials, you not only make a positive impact but also open doors to new opportunities and a broader client base.

CHAPTER 3
THE STRUGGLE IS REAL

"Where there is no struggle, there is absolutely no progress." - Eric Thomas

---

I remember when I first wanted to become a real estate agent. It was going to be so fun and glamorous. I'd be able to show gorgeous homes, help people, and have loads of free time! What a great combination! At least, that's what they lead us to believe on television! Ha! Now I want to be clear, I didn't decide to become an agent after watching Million-Dollar Listing, but I have to admit I was a little disappointed when real life wasn't anything like what they portray on my favorite reality shows. What they don't tell you on TV, is how unglamorous, challenging, and stressful this industry can be.

. . .

Even if you've been in it for years, you never know where the next lead is coming from. It feels impossible to know how much income you'll make each year, and in addition to that, the liability, difficult clients, and being "on-call" all the time can quickly make any new real estate career lose its luster. Another thing I didn't realize at first, is that the market is saturated with agents. For many new agents, it can be a real struggle to figure out how to differentiate yourself and convey why strangers should choose YOU to help them buy or sell a home over the top agent in their neighborhood.

I mention all of this so that you know, I understand what it's like to be a struggling agent. Through my experience and from talking with my agent friends, there are two main reasons why beginning and growing a real estate business is challenging.

- Most people don't want to be perceived as a sales guy
- Most people don't like to cold call

So, the idea of reading sales scripts or knocking on doors and asking everyone you know for referrals is cringeworthy. However, the traditional ways to grow your real estate business all include doing things that your mind keeps saying no to, like:

- Calling your sphere to ask for referrals
- Join groups to network with people, so you can ask for referrals
- Market yourself on social media, provide transactional guidance, and ask for business
- Door knock and ask for referrals.

That's a whole lot of asking and not very much giving! I think that is why it can be so hard as a new single agent. If you are lucky enough to be on a supportive team with a top-selling mentor, then please know you are blessed, because that's not the case for most new agents.

Since most real estate agents are also small business owners, there is a whole lot of extra "stuff" that you'll need to know how to do: marketing, lead generation, sales, account management, accounting, oh yeah, and then all the real estate transaction stuff too. That's a whole lot to learn! And it's a lot to expect that one person will be really good at all of these things right away. So if you feel like you sometimes struggle with your business, give yourself a break, and don't be so hard on yourself! Be proud that you are taking steps to learn more and find ways to grow your business. Just take it baby step by baby step, and if you keep it up, you'll be running in no time.

TRADITIONAL REAL ESTATE MARKETING

So, let's talk about marketing because that's my specialty, and I feel like it's where most agents could use a little help. There are several ways to market yourself and your business, and many agents simply call their business Jane Doe real estate or Jane Doe homes and get started. There's nothing wrong with that, but I do believe that there is a better way. (Suggestions for the better way to market yourself are explored in chapter 5.)

Let's look at some of the tools we use to market ourselves.

- **Social media** - Using tools like Facebook, Instagram, LinkedIN, and now even TikTok are incredible free tools that every agent should be using to grow their following. In fact, many consumers will check your social media account even before they go to your website!
- **Direct Mail** - Direct Mail marketing can be a very powerful tool IF you have the funds to pay for it. Doing a one-time print campaign may have little to no effect because it will take repeated mailings consistently over 6, 12 or 18 months before agents will start seeing leads come in solely

from direct mail campaigns. AND the message you print is key. Sending junk mail is a waste of money, so be sure what you mail provides value and differentiates you as well. In any case, direct mail may not be a viable option for newer agents, but can be very powerful for an agent who can afford to send regular print media to their sphere, neighborhood or even their local preferred zip codes. I do have a solution for this that I'll explain in chapter 5.

- **Person-to-person** - This is the best and most direct form of marketing yourself. Person-to-person conversations, whether they are on the phone, on zoom, or live, give you the highest conversion or lead generation because you are connecting with people about your business. The conversation can evolve organically, and you can overcome objections as they come up. The biggest problem is that most agents don't know what to say to people.
- **Paid advertising** - Like print marketing, paid advertising can be a costly investment that may take several months before it starts "working". And if your message isn't resonating with potential clients, it could feel like a big waste of money.
- **Buying Leads** - Gone are the days when you could pay for Zillow Premier Agent and then sit back and watch the leads roll in. The amount of leads you get depends on how saturated your

market is and the demand of buyers and sellers who don't already have an agent, so it could pay off or be a waste of money.

Why Traditional Methods Don't Work For Everyone

The main reason why traditional methods of marketing produce little to no results is not because of the method. **It's because of your message**. If you aren't saying anything different, then you are saying the same thing all agents say. "I'll help you find your dream home, or I'm number one, or I know the community really well, or I'm a great negotiator." The fact is that you are a real estate agent and most consumers expect that you will know the community well and that you know how to negotiate a sale.

Most people think all agents are the same.

If you meet someone and they say, "what do you do for a living?" and you say, "I'm a real estate agent." Usually, the conversation is over, and in their mind, they lump you with all the other realtors they already know. They automatically judge you as good or bad based on their past experiences and beliefs. So even if you are a "friend", if they don't know how you are different or why you are the better agent of choice, when it comes time to sell or buy a home, they probably will not choose you. Unless you are a direct relative they are trying to help, most sellers will hire the agent who does the most business in their neighborhood, and most buyers will work with an agent who was referred to them, rather than their "friends". People want to make a logical choice and not choose among their friends. So if you don't talk about your business with people, how will they even know anything about the value you offer?

THE SECRET AGENT IS BORN

I've known many "secret agents" over the years; you know, those acquaintances that you've known for a long time that never talk about their business? They never ask for referrals, and they never post anything about work except for the occasional SOLD post on social media. Is that you? It was me before I found wellness real estate!

I believe many people become secret agents simply because they don't want to seem "salesy" or pushy. They cringe at saying, "Do you know anyone looking to buy or sell?" If the conversation isn't naturally leading that way, how awkward is it to ask that question out of the blue? Secret agents don't want to be associated with salespeople who try to "close" their friends and random people they meet. They also might have the belief that it looks desperate to ask for referrals a lot. Ultimately, what makes these people Secret Agents is that they never talk about their real estate business.

Stealth Mode

So, how do you talk about your business, without really talking about your business? Are you going to be "that person" who always seems to bring the conversation around to real estate and the market?

For those who are thinking of buying or selling, it's great, but for those who aren't, it's just annoying. I know for sure I was a secret agent because I didn't want to be that "annoying friend."

I don't know about you, but most of my friends know about 5-10 real estate agents they like and trust personally. If it's the same for you, how will you stand out? I love to use this analogy from Seth Godin's book Purple Cow: Imagine driving down a country road and seeing beautiful countryside, the sun is shining, and you see a ranch with a whole herd of cows. You might say, " Wow, look at those cool cows!" You might even look at them as you drive past and try to see how many there are. Then you keep going, and you see another herd, and another herd, and so on. So, you stop paying attention to them, and after a while, you don't even notice they're there. But what if you keep driving and see a purple cow? Wow! You'd stop and take notice then, wouldn't you? It's so different! It's unique! It makes you look *because* it stands out.

I'm here to encourage you to think about how you can be a purple cow in your business.

Now imagine being at a neighborhood event and you were able to captivate and engage a circle of people you just met with real estate-related topics that highlight your expertise in sort of a ninja-subtle way. It is possible! And wellness real estate is the brilliant ninja technique that helps you get there. It's brilliant because no one is talking about wellness real estate, so it's new news. Also, everyone wants to be healthy, so it's engaging! And it's ninja because the conversation is so fun they don't even realize they are talking about real estate or learning about your business!

Wellness real estate is an entirely new concept that most people have never heard of. It's unique and engaging, and most people will be surprised and even impressed with what is currently taking place across the country! The point is that you don't have to be a secret agent anymore, and you don't have to be a "salesy agent" that attends events to find out who needs to sell their home.

According to recent reports1[5], there has been a substantial and noticeable increase in consumer prioritization of wellness over the past two or three years. "79% of people say that wellness is important, and 42% of them consider it a top priority." So why not educate your audience on what is happening in the industry? Why not share the news of wellness in real estate? Why not help your clients learn how they can create a healthier home environment? Why not surround yourself with healthy home experts you can collaborate with and connect with your clients?

That's all you need to do to start differentiating yourself from the sea of agents who are helping people find their "dream home." Help people find a healthy home instead because no one is doing that, and ultimately that's what people really want anyway.

―――――

LET WELLNESS REAL ESTATE BE THE BRIDGE THAT CONNECTS YOU TO MORE PEOPLE

> "The residential real estate market is the next frontier that will be radically transformed by the wellness movement. The way our homes have been built in the last century is reinforcing unhealthy lifestyles that make us sick, stressed, alienated and unhappy." - Global Wellness Institute

What if you could be more than a transaction facilitator? What if you could stop attracting those difficult clients, the ones that drain your energy emotionally and physically? What if there was a way you could attract clients that are more like you and could help others in a more meaningful way that lines up with your values? What if you could do more and be more without actually having to work more? That's the dream, right? If we keep doing business the same, how can we expect any dramatic change? Unless we change. Change our approach, change our perspective, change our tactics, change our intensity or frequency, you can pick any one you like, but something has to change if you want change. So what is it that you can change? Let this question stay in the back of your mind as you finish reading this book and then come back to it.

We all know health and wellness is big business, and everyone is prioritizing health and wellness in their purchases and their travel plans now, more than ever. What I've learned is that there is so much more that goes into health and well-being besides diet and exercise. All the stuff off your plate, like finances, relationships, and your home environment, are other important factors directly affecting your overall well-being. Also important are your feelings of self-worth, the need to feel like you matter, and the desire you have to use all your talents and skills. The more of these aspects going well in your life, the better you feel. On the other hand, if any of these elements are toxic, such as a toxic workplace or relationship, or if you are living in a toxic home environment, these will all lead to an increase in stress and a decline in physical well-being.

It's time we learn how to take a holistic approach to healthier living, and as agents, we can help our clients do that.

I encourage you to become a CONNECTOR who creates an expanded network of healthy home experts who can offer solutions to your community to help them thrive.

Sharing your values, bringing people together, and helping others live better lives will bring you more fulfillment and meaning because it's aligned with who you really are. It's attracting like-minded people to you and working from the inside out.

What it's going to take is an agent who cares about the health and wellness of their clients and wants to make a difference. Be the agent who is a forward thinker and isn't afraid to approach things differently. Stay current in the changing marketplace because we all know businesses that thrive are the ones who adapt to change. People will be searching for a healthier home, especially once they realize it is available to them.

So what's the one thing you can do?

Position yourself to be the one that brings them that option.

There's never been a time better than now to educate yourself on what your future customers will ask you. Be the innovator and the thought leader in your community. I'm on a mission to make this world a healthier place, one home at a time, and I invite you to join me.

WHAT IT MEANS TO BE A CHANGE AGENT

There are a lot of ways you can be an agent for change. Even if your goal isn't to become a public speaker or be involved at the government level, you still can become a leader in your circle of friends, in your small groups, and in your community. More on this is in chapter 5.

- **Support industry-wide improvements.** Whether it's government policies or a new community being built in the area, look for ways to communicate and educate the positive aspects of these improvements to others. People can often have an immediate negative reaction to change, and they want to fight and complain about everything. This never helps. Be a positive person who embraces change and improvements, this mindset helps everyone.
- **Look for wellness lifestyle communities near you** and go visit them. Share what you learn with others.
- **Support local businesses that align with your values and brand.** Collaborate with them, showcase them on your website, and post or send an email about your favorite places to eat, shop, and play in your community.
- **Connect and network with healthy home professionals and help share what they teach.** In turn, you will be essentially educating your audience about wellness in real estate. Offer them simple strategies to create a healthier home environment. How to detect mold, how to

improve air quality, where to go to test their water, and showcase your favorite home improvement projects and products that have helped you.

The NAR's Green Resource Council states that homebuyers will pay on average 9-13% more for a home with green features. These are just documented green features, not even features that support health and wellness. They also say that buyers prefer green over non-green amenities when given a choice. That trend is only going to grow. How will they know about these amenities if no one is educating them?

CHAPTER 4
SIMPLE STRATEGIES TO PROVIDE MORE VALUE

"Be the change you want to see in the world." - Gandhi

This chapter will help you learn simple strategies that engage your audience and provide more value. But what exactly is value? **Value is giving something your audience wants.** The tricky part about this is similar to the organic movement when it first began, people weren't asking for organic in the beginning. However now that people realize there are options for them and they understand the toxicity that is abundant in conventional farming, people can make more informed decisions. Likewise, I doubt that your clients are asking for a "healthy home". But as the demand for wellness increases and people realize that there are options for them to improve air quality beyond replacing HEPA filters and that mold is not something to dismiss, or that whole house water filtration is a wise investment, they too will start asking more questions. And the agents who are connected and prepared will shoot to the top.

But just for a moment, let's step back and think about traditional real estate marketing or education for a moment. Most agents provide value by supplying transaction advice and support or community or property-focused support. And don't get me wrong that is necessary and a very important part of being a real estate agent, but if all you talk about is real estate news or listings and open houses, it gets pretty boring for someone who's not looking to move. At least they see that you are working, but that doesn't give them a real reason to hire you. You can only talk about interest rates or the latest home you visited so many times with the same person before they might start running the other way when they see you coming. Yikes, no one wants that.

One of the problems agents encounter today is the super-informed consumer who may believe they know the market better than anyone. With information available at their fingertips online, that might very well be true, yet consumers still want to hire professionals who they feel know more about real estate than they do. They do not understand the liability issues or the transactional headaches that come with buying and selling a home. All they know is that they can look up the price per square foot sold listings on Zillow pretty easily. Unfortunately, all this information has empowered the consumer and strengthened their belief that agents aren't worth the cost of hiring one. So instead of lowering your fees or working for a discount broker, why not *show* them the value you offer?

To provide value to your clients, you must have information that is important to them that they can not find or do not already know themselves. And you must share this information with people before they hire you. Sharing this information regularly is how you build trust and how you position yourself as an expert.

For example, if negotiations are your strong suit, then you should post and email and tell stories about how you have won negotiations. Offer strategies and showcase negotiation mistakes home sellers or buyers often make. Likewise, if you decide that you want to talk about wellness real estate with people, then you will want to post, email, and talk to people about this topic. Introduce them to healthy home experts in your area and become the go-to resource in your community for healthy homes.

> **It's not about you becoming the healthy home expert. It's about you being the connector to the experts.**

Networking and promoting this expanded group of home professionals will set you apart and the one who "knows" how to create or find a healthy home or someone who understands the "value" of these types of upgrades when it's time to sell.

So how can you connect and get more engagement, stay top of mind, and bring value to those around you? A well-planned marketing strategy and a clear message will get you there.

You can start by thinking about your ideal client's potential questions and then answering them in your posts. For example, if you have sold to many first-time home buyers and want to attract more, doing a first-time homebuyer workshop and posting about things they need to qualify for a home is super helpful!

If you want to specialize in luxury homes in your area, sharing information on all the gated neighborhoods and what makes them unique would be helpful. This kind of information is hard to find, so it's valuable to someone looking for a home in a gated community. Maybe you're a dog lover; you could post about the local dog parks or dog-friendly restaurants in your area. These are just a few examples of the practical value you can provide that positions you as the neighborhood expert.

Sell Benefits, not Features

You might be thinking this all sounds great, but "My clients never ask for green homes or healthy homes, so why should I care?" The reason people don't directly ask for "green homes" or "healthy homes" is that people don't usually ask for features; they ask for results or benefits. They may not even know that "green homes" are something you can search for on the MLS. They may not know that there is even such a thing as a healthy home search.

Selling green and wellness will resonate if you speak to their pain points and highlight the benefits they will receive, instead of pointing out features they don't understand. For example, If you have a headache and someone is trying to sell you something to help with dehydration, you probably wouldn't pay any attention even if that's the cause of your headache. You want something that will help your throbbing head. Likewise, if I started talking to you about SEER ratings for air conditioners or R-values for insulation, it won't be long before your eyes glaze over and your mind starts wandering. But if I pointed out the potential monthly savings on your utility bill and how much more comfortable you'll be upstairs in the summer heat, you may pay more attention. And if I am the person who connects you with the best HVAC company that saves you money and provides you peace of mind and comfort, then I can give myself a high five because I bet you will remember that too. If I do this a couple of times, you may even start referring to me as "your agent". Sweet! That's what we want!

When properly marketed, buyers do want "green" and wellness. After all, who doesn't want to live in a more comfortable home that has modern conveniences, fewer toxins, is mold-free and saves them money on their utility bills each month? In fact, as I mentioned earlier, NAR's Green Resource Council states that "homebuyers will pay on average 9-13% more for a home with green features." Now, imagine adding healthy home features to the list!

You might be thinking: if I specialize in wellness real estate, doesn't that mean I will lose business because not every home is a wellness home? The answer is, of course, not! Your marketing message is simply the message you project to everyone so that you can attract your ideal clients. You can always help whomever you want. This is not about naming homes wellness homes or healthy homes either. It's not about selling just green homes. It's about expanding your knowledge and network. Period. It's about being more than you are now. It's about adding value to what you do now, not limiting yourself.

The bottom line is if you have picked up this book and read it this far, it's likely that you are passionate about healthy living and the idea of wellness in real estate sounds very intriguing. This is great news! All I'm suggesting is that you open your marketing mind and see all the possibilities of networking and education you can take advantage of to help foster a better community and grow your brand and business in the process.

Simple Truths

Here's the truth: fear in your subconscious mind will tell you to stay in your comfort zone, that this sounds hooky and has nothing to do with selling real estate. If that's you, know that is just your mind being uncomfortable with change and uncertainty and it's completely normal. I would suggest that you continue reading this book with an open mind and see if there are any nuggets that you can take away to implement in your business. Like for example, start talking about this book with some of your friends who are in your sphere and just hear their reactions. Pay attention to how easy and authentic you are being at the same time you are talking about your business. Wellness real estate really is the bridge to having more conversations about your business!

Here's another truth: Most agents are marketing themselves the same. They all say the same things and do the same things. How many agents can be #1 really? How often have you heard "I can help you find your dream home, or sell yours faster for more money?" Isn't it time to say something unique? After all, your marketing message isn't about who you'll say yes or no to, it's about attracting your ideal client to you. Sharing the values that are important to you and sharing yourself in your marketing is you being authentic and that attracts like-minded people to you! Picture a scenario where you exclusively collaborate with clients you genuinely enjoy working with, and who share your passions and values. That's the power of attraction. When you market to everyone or say the same thing everyone is saying, no one pays attention. It's too vague, it doesn't stand out, so your message is ignored, and you end up working hard and helping no one.

For example, if I ran an ad campaign that says "I can help you lose weight" vs. "keto recipes that help you lose 10 pounds in 3 days", which ad do you think will get more clicks? Sure, it will be people interested in Keto, not just anyone wanting to lose weight, but if you are a keto diet coach, isn't that even better?

· · ·

So instead of saying what everyone says about helping clients sell faster for more money or helping them find their dream home, what if you asked if their energy upgrades are included in the ROI when it comes time to sell? See how that is more inviting? It is conversational and interesting, and positions you as a leader with an opportunity to educate and add value. That post is much more helpful, and it will attract your ideal client.

Here's how you can start creating a better marketing plan that clearly defines and articulates what you do and attracts your audience to you. I have also created a workbook that will help you go through these steps that you can find at https://www.healthyhomemedia.com/wellnessrebook

MARKETING ADVICE

Define your target audience

If you could have mostly one type of client who would that be? Of course, we would never discriminate or turn people away, but if you have sold mostly downtown condos to young professionals and say you want to specialize in suburban gated communities because that's where you live, then you should change your marketing to speak to families that want to live in those neighborhoods rather than just sharing the condos you've sold downtown.

· · ·

Define your values

What is important to you? What values do you hold dear to your heart?

Reflecting on your values is crucial because they can be powerful elements in your marketing strategy. When you incorporate your genuine beliefs into your posts and emails, your communication becomes authentic and relatable. By speaking your truth and sharing what truly matters to you, your messages resonate deeply. This authenticity naturally attracts people who align with your values, fostering genuine connections.

Develop your personal brand

This is more than picking your colors and logo design. It's a deeper look into what you want your name and your personal brand to represent. What do you want to be known for? What do you want to help people with most of all? If you couldn't name your business, your name, what would it be? Is your brand just about your neighborhood? Or is there something more?

Write your one-liner

A good one-liner intrigues people instead of boring them, so they will continue the conversation and begin asking questions to learn more!

. . .

To craft a one-liner that hooks your audience, you'll need 3 parts:

- part one: the problem your client faces
- part two: the solution your product or service offers
- part three: the results your clients get by using your service or product.

Here are a couple of examples of mine to help get your ideas flowing:

HealthyHOME™ Media offers custom-branded wellness lifestyle magazines for real estate agents that bridge the gap between transactions and heartfelt connections so you can spend less time creating marketing materials and more time connecting with people.

and/or

I am a publisher and digital marketer, and I create unique custom-branded marketing tools for real estate agents and healthy home professionals that enable them to engage and connect with more people authentically about their business.

Self-Reflect

What is your current mindset? What is your self-talk like normally? Do you find yourself talking yourself out of good ideas? Do you have beliefs that limit you? Becoming self-aware is the first step to creating positive change in your life. If you find that you feel stuck more often than not, take time each day to self-reflect and meditate. Don't rehash negative stories simply ask yourself "what beliefs do I have that are holding me back?" and then let that go and meditate. Quiet your mind and just listen to soft music or repeat "let go" over and over in your head so you stop "thinking". It gets easier the more you practice, and you'll find that you'll become more aware when your negative beliefs come up. Once they do, you can ask yourself if this belief is always true for everyone 100% of the time, and since the answer will be no, you can tell yourself something softer instead, like "I'm getting better, things are changing, I don't need that belief anymore because it doesn't serve me." In time, you'll let that go and will be able to allow more opportunities to flow into your life!

An amazing book I just read that I highly recommend and can help in this area is a NY Times Bestseller called "Stress Less, Accomplish More" by Emily Fletcher

Define What You Want

Imagine walking up to an airline ticket booth and saying "I want to travel." The agent will ask you, "where do you want to go?" When we say "I want more money, or I want my business to be successful," we are being too vague. We need to specifically ask for what we want. This helps us take action steps to achieve actual trackable goals instead of vague ones. Take a moment to write down 10 specific goals you want to accomplish this year, then see if you can reverse engineer the baby steps it will take to achieve them.

Marketing Ideas

Having a clear, compelling message is not just beneficial; it's a game-changer for your business. Having a clear unique message sets you apart and it resonates with your target audience which means it attracts clients who align with your values. Think of it as the beacon that guides potential clients to your expertise. By crafting a message that is unique and that people can easily understand, you not only define what you stand for but also gain clarity for yourself on what your brand represents. This clarity becomes your strength, empowering you to showcase the extra knowledge and network you've gained from this book. It's not just about what you do; it's about how you help your clients. Doing any one of these strategies will begin to transform your marketing approach, setting you on a path to connect with the right clients effortlessly and authentically.

Here are some out-of-the-box marketing ideas for you to consider:

- Create a local podcast

The best way to market yourself is to look for more ways to talk about your business and how you help people. For me, that has been through podcasting! It's simple, it's free, and you don't have to get dressed up! You can read a script and record it any time of the day or night. Having a podcast allows you to showcase local business owners, and your network of experts, which benefits everyone. It helps your audience, it helps your network and it helps you! Plus when you give free press to a local business and let the owner talk about what they do and how they help, you just made a new friend! Create a free podcast at www.anchor.fm

- Create an Instagram or TikTok show

Similar to podcasting, you can interview local business owners and your team of experts that you network with on your "show". It doesn't have to a long interview, it can be as simple as one or two questions and a call to action!

- Create a Newsletter

You can also highlight local businesses and home experts in a newsletter you send to your email list each month. This is where you can share articles you find on the internet about wellness real estate too!

- Use polls and ask questions in your social media feed and stories to engage your audience

- Host Events or Learning Workshops

Host events that bring people together to either learn something new that you teach them or bring in an expert to do the teaching. Healthy cooking would a fun event, or hire a photographer to take pictures of families before the holidays as an added treat. Or host an event for a client who has recently bought a home and invite their neighbors to attend. You can start a doggie playtime for your neighborhood and bring dog snacks so all the dog owners can meet each other. Or perhaps you could consider hosting a workshop for potential home buyers or sellers, centered around the concept of healthy homes. This unique angle could serve as a compelling hook to engage your audience. Imagine this "Unlock the Secret to Healthy Homes: Join Our Exclusive Workshop for Home Buyers and Sellers! Discover How Your Home Choices Can Enhance Your Well-being and Transform Your Lifestyle."

- Give Thoughtful Gifts

You know, giving a thoughtful gift doesn't have to break the bank. How about sending a heartfelt handwritten note to show your appreciation? Or maybe you could share some local goodies, like artisanal chocolates or coffee, that reflect the charm of your area. Another idea could be crafting something personal, like homemade scented candles or unique coasters. And hey, if they're into reading, why not share an interesting e-book or online course? It's these little gestures that really make a difference and show you care.

Here's a golden tip: make sure your gifts align with your brand and what you want to be known for. Instead of going for generic presents, pay attention during your interactions. Listen to their interests, their hobbies, what makes them tick. It could be as simple as a book related to their passion or a local delicacy you discussed during your meeting. These thoughtful, personalized gifts not only show you care but also leave a lasting impression, making your connection even more memorable.

MARKETING BOOKS WORTH THE READ

Here is a list of some great books that will help you define your message and grow your brand and a couple extra that will help you relax so your good ideas keep flowing.

- Building a Story Brand, by Don Miller

- Primal branding, by Patrick Hanlon
- The ONE Thing, by Gary Keller
- Miracle Morning for Real Estate Agents, by Michael J. Maher
- Stress Less, Accomplish More, by Emily Fletcher

CHAPTER 5

THE WELLNESS ADVANTAGE: ELEVATING YOUR REAL ESTATE BRAND

"Just as ripples spread out when a single pebble is dropped into water, the actions of individuals can have far-reaching effects." - Dalai Lama

In today's fast-paced real estate landscape, embracing a wellness-focused approach isn't just a trend; it's a powerful strategy that can transform your career through heartfelt connections. In this chapter, we'll explore simple yet highly effective strategies that, when incorporated, not only enhance your clients' lives but also elevate your position in the industry. These actionable steps offer a roadmap to infuse wellness seamlessly into your real estate business, ensuring not just success, but a deeply fulfilling and purpose-driven journey.

It's important to note that you can share healthy home tips with your followers *without* rebranding yourself as a Wellness REALTOR®.

> There are many agents that I work with who have been established professionals for years who prefer to simply share their values by stating that "I am passionate about healthy living, and so I've expanded my knowledge and network to provide you with resources that will help your family live more joyfully in your home."

On the other hand, there are many agents who choose this topic as a way to differentiate themselves in their marketing, and I have compiled a long list of examples you'll find later in this chapter. I encourage you to do your own research and reach out and connect with these forward-thinking agents yourself. I've met them all and know they will be more than delighted to share with you their story and how it has helped them expand their reach and elevate their brand. So whether you want to call yourself a Holistic REALTOR®, Wellness Agent, Wellness-Focused Agent, Regenerative, Green or Eco-agent, or none of the above, the label doesn't matter. The message and the brand identity you want to cultivate are key. I created a workbook on developing your personal brand, and you can download it free on my website at https://www.healthyhomemedia.com/wellnessrebook

STARTING AUTHENTIC CONVERSATIONS: WELLNESS REAL ESTATE IS YOUR BRIDGE

Start talking about the wellness real estate news you find online. Follow the Global Wellness Institute, and check out my podcast, The Wellness Real Estate podcast. I interview different home wellness experts and industry leaders, and we talk about all sorts of things, from green mortgages to wool insulation. I also interview developers of wellness communities and other wellness agents who share how they do business differently.

I have created a FREE pdf of some simple conversation starters that will inspire you to have more easy-flowing conversations about wellness real estate and your business. If you'd like a copy, head on over to my website https://www.healthyhomemedia.com/wellnessrebook and you can download it for free.

SHARE AND EDUCATE ONLINE

Share wellness real estate news, trends, and tips on your social media, email, and in the conversations, you have with people. Imagine how helpful you will be by sharing information about creating a healthier home. All it takes is a quick search, and you can find numerous blog posts and articles on home toxins, eco-design, color psychology, biophilic design, Feng Shui, green building, etc. It allows you to have endless content that is much more interesting and engaging than if you only post about your listings. Sprinkle this info in with your market updates and listings, and you will be providing value instead of just selling.

I have created 30 social media ideas to help get you started. Simply head to my website https://www.healthyhomemedia.com/wellnessrebook and you can download the pdf for free.

NETWORK

Network with green service providers and healthy home experts in your area. I said this before in the earlier chapter but it's important to reemphasize here:

It's not about you becoming the healthy home expert. It's about you being the connector to the experts.

As a real estate agent you are already the connector for people who help in a real estate transaction, so it's only natural for you to expand your network so you can refer your clients to experts for everything home. Expanding your network creates a wonderful opportunity for you to learn new things you can share, and helps the other business owners since you are sharing what they do with your audience. You might come up with new ways to collaborate and do events together or promote each other's businesses.

Here are some home wellness experts you may want in your network:

- Biophilic Designer
- Building Biology Practitioner to test for other toxins
- Color Psychology Specialist
- Eco Designers and Green Home Stagers
- Energy Auditor that can perform a blower door test
- Feng Shui Consultant
- HVAC Contractor that understands HRV and ERV systems
- Green Appraiser - Green Builder / Wellness Architect
- Green/Healthy Home Builder and Contractor
- Green Lenders (those who have access to green mortgage programs)
- Green Home Supply (www.thegreendesigncenter.com)

- Home Inspector who understands healthy homes
- Mold Inspector that tests more than the air
- Mold Remediation Company
- Non-toxic Pest Services (orange oil termite service)
- Other Wellness Agents to collaborate and refer
- Solar Consultant
- Water Filtration company

I've created a Healthy Home checklist that you can give your clients after closing or even to your buyers when they are searching for a home. You can download it free, and I'll even send you the Canva template so you can brand it with your own information and not have to start from scratch! It's a great place to list some of the business partners in your network, and your clients will keep it for future reference! Simply head to https://www.healthyhomemedia.com/wellnessrebook to grab that for yourself.

STAND OUT WITH THESE PROFESSIONAL ACCREDITATIONS AND DESIGNATIONS

Some agents are diving deep into these certifications to educate themselves in order to be able to help their clients on a deeper level. Here are some to check out:

- According to the US Green Building Council, "A LEED credential denotes proficiency in today's sustainable design, construction, and operations standards. More than 203,000 professionals have earned a LEED credential to help advance their careers. Showcase your knowledge, experience, and credibility in the green building marketplace as a LEED professional." They have 2 credentials professionals can earn, LEED Green Associate, and LEED AP with specialty.
- Energy Star Partner Programs give professionals the opportunity to gain education and to become accredited service providers and/or have products energy star certified.
- Fitwell Ambassador is a credential given to professionals who go through their specific training to gain leading-edge industry knowledge and further their careers. According to Fitwell "the business case for health-promoting real estate has never been stronger."
- The Living Future Institute has many different online courses to choose from to further your education on sustainable and healthy design for the built environment.
- The Well Building Institute offers accreditation for professionals to become a Well AP. Professionals gain a competitive edge as an accredited health and well-being expert with the WELL AP designation that differentiates them

and connects them to over 21,000 other Well AP professionals around the world.

GET INVOLVED

There are lots of ways you can get more involved to network and learn from others. The benefits of taking this step opens your world to a whole new group of people that can inspire you to new ideas and opportunities for your business. So I encourage you to do some research and see what groups seem interesting to you. Take that first step of visiting and checking it out before you commit to anything, but be open to getting involved. You can always limit how much time this involvement will be, but opening your world to new people and experiences is how we grow!

- Research your Local MLS Association or NAR Association for opportunities to join or create a Holistic, Green, Sustainable or Healthy Living group
- Create a Wellness Real Estate group within your brokerage so you can generate camaraderie and support within your real estate agent community.
- Research and join Facebook groups
- Follow other wellness agents on Facebook and Instagram.

- We want to connect you with other forward-thinking industry professionals, to be a part of our tribe, to collaborate, connect, and to refer! Join our free Facebook group at www.facebook.com/groups/wellnessre

USE THESE RESOURCES

Over the years, I've learned about some pretty great resources for real estate professionals who want to differentiate themselves and their listings. Here are few of them:

- The NAR GREEN Designation is available to National Association of REALTOR® members. Agents who take their additional courses online or in person that focus on selling homes with energy-efficient features gain a better understanding of the special care that should be given to these properties and become GREEN Designees upon completion.
- A Pearl Certification helps homeowners quantify the value of their energy-efficient features when it's time to sell. It is intended for homeowners or listing agents and provides a certification plus marketing tools so potential buyers can understand the benefits of the home's energy-efficient features. They have certifications for

solar only as well as home, and there are different levels that can be achieved.
- Realtysage is like a Zillow for green homes. They evaluate all the different certifications of various properties and use their innovative comparison tool, which assigns each listing a Sage Score for better understanding. Agents can upload their listings free and become Realtysage preferred agents to earn referrals as well!
- HealthyHOME Media is the company I started in 2020. We create custom-branded wellness lifestyle magazines that enable agents to authentically engage with more people about their business.

LIVE IT

People can sense if you are being authentic or not, so it's really important that you live what you believe. If you plan to position yourself as a wellness real estate professional means that you care about living healthier in your own home environment. So share what you are doing to create a healthier home. When you declutter, share that on your social media. When you paint and choose a brand that offers low or no-VOC choices, share that with your audience too! When you start being the leader, people who resonate with what you are doing will follow.

HOME™ Magazine. Learn more at www.balancedarchitecture.com

DESIGN WELL STUDIOS

Michelle Ifversen is an environmental wellness designer in Portland, Oregon, specializing in biophilic design. Biophilic Design is all about bringing nature in as a design element within built environments to increase occupant connectivity and overall well-being. It's a concept widely used in commercial spaces, but Michelle Ifversen, the founder of Design Well Studios, is blazing a trail to bring biophilic design into our homes. Her firm is an environmental wellness design and testing company that optimizes built environments that promote beauty, health, and well-being. They offer state-of-the-art, professional environmental testing services that allow their clients to see if their home or workplace has issues from poor air or water quality, mold or high levels of EMFs that could negatively affect their health. Through education and their creative design hacks, as well as products and services, they help remedy spaces so people can thrive. Michelle has an extensive blog and also is a regular contributing writer for my publications, Wellness Real Estate Magazine™ and HealthyHOME™ Magazine. Learn more at www.designwellstudios.com

GREEN BUILDING MAP

Pino Fortunado is a real estate agent in Manhattan, NY. Born in Italy, he came to the United States as the Founder and Executive Director of EcoArt Project, a nonprofit organization on a mission to stimulate climate change action and environmental awareness by leveraging the creativity of artists and designers. Being an active advocate for community and environmental wellness, he could see how there was a need in the real estate industry to showcase the many buildings in Manhattan that were making efforts to retrofit or become green-certified. Seeing that need, he created an incredible online tool called GreenBuildingMap.com. The mapping app locates green-certified residential and commercial properties and features green architecture, design, and technology components. This Green Building Map is a game-changer that makes the real estate community more transparent. Pino is also the founder of Wellness Real Estate Advisory, a national network of real estate professionals, industry experts, and specialized companies working in this niche market. The latest program Pino has launched with his nonprofit is called Rebound-NYC. The initiative repurposes empty storefronts in New York City into transformative temporary pop-up art experiences. It aims to beautify and revitalize the city by empowering artists through curated exhibitions and experiences and commissioned performances. Not only is Pino's work supporting local artists, it's also bringing life back to spaces that need it the most after a challenging year of battling the COVID-19 pandemic. How amazing!! Learn more at www.greenbuildingmap.com

GREEN HOME COACH

Marla Esser Cloos, otherwise known as the Green Home Coach, helps homeowners and real estate agents better understand how to navigate creating a healthier and greener home environment. She has a podcast, books and courses designed to make learning simple and easy. Learn more at www.greenhomecoach.com

GREEN HOMEOWNERS UNITED

Kevin Kane is the Chief Economist and Strategist for Green Homeowners United in Madison, Wisconsin. He was the first homebuyer in his town to use a green mortgage when purchasing his first home, and he used it to upgrade old appliances, windows, new heating and cooling systems, as well as to add solar to the existing home. It was a challenging experience for him since no one knew exactly who to call or how to guide him through the process. After seeing the value of his home increase while reaping the benefits of a more comfortable home and lower utility bills, he decided he would help others do the same. He has been educating homeowners in Wisconsin about the benefits of a green mortgage and networking with lenders across the country to provide these programs in every state.

Kevin connects with wellness-focused real estate agents around the country so they too can share this message and help more people with green mortgages. If you'd like to learn more, go to https://www.greenhomewi.com/

HEALTHY HOUSE ON THE BLOCK

Amanda Klecker is a Certified Home Inspector and Certified Building Biology Advocate in Minneapolis, Minnesota. She helps homeowners and real estate agents around the country with practical solutions and research-based advice for creating healthy indoor spaces. As a mother, Amanda wanted to provide a safe and healthy home for her children and believes that a home can be a refuge from health-limiting toxins in our everyday world. She is trained to identify and help homeowners make smart decisions regarding a home purchase and she assists agents so they understand problems and can better guide their clients. As a green living expert, Amanda has published an extensive blog and provides personal services that educate clients on toxins with science-backed research, so they feel empowered to make small changes in their own home environment. Amanda has an extensive blog and also is a regular contributing writer for my publications, Wellness Real Estate Magazine™ and Healthy-HOME™ Magazine. Learn more at www.healthyhouseontheblock.com

· · ·

LATITUDE

Neal and Alissa Collins are real estate agents in the Pacific Northwest. Originally from Portland, Oregon, they now reside in Whidbey Island, Washington. They have started a movement that they have coined Regenerative Real Estate and have boldly marketed that message on their podcast and through social media. Agents from around the country have resonated with their message and have joined their eXp brokerage, Latitude, or their affiliate group of change agents.

Together, they bring new conversations to real estate that intersect with sustainability and ecology. Learn more at www.chooselatitude.com

SMART LIVING HAWAII

Christina Laney Mitre is the founder of Smart Living Hawaii, a non-profit organization that aims to be a resource and community hub for Hawaii's sustainable Energy, Agriculture, Environment, Housing, and Culture sectors. As a NAR GREEN Designee and WellnessRE™PRO, she has taken an active role at a state and association level to help bring difficult conversations to the table and drive solutions that will bring positive change to her community. Through her Smart Living Hawaii Podcast, she brings in local business leaders who share their insights on sustainability, home technology, and energy savings as well as healthy lifestyle. Learn more at www.smartlivinghi.org

THE GREEN DESIGN CENTER

Andrew Pace is a Healthy Home Concierge and Founder of The Green Design Center, a leading resource for homeowners and contractors looking to source products that are healthy and green and receive expert consulting advice on designing and building healthy green homes. Andrew is the host of the weekly Non Toxic Environments Podcast. He is a worldwide expert on green and healthy building products and services for customers and contractors from around the globe. As founder of the oldest healthy building supply company in the United States, Andrew has become one of the single most helpful and educational experts dealing with the day-to-day concerns of those individuals who suffer from allergies, asthma and chemical sensitivities. Learn more at www.thegreendesigncenter.com

WELLNESS BY DEZIGN

Cassy West is a LEED v4 Green Associate, Fitwell Ambassador, Wellness Within Your Walls Certified, a NAR GREEN Designee, a WellnessRE™PRO and she's certified in healthy building materials serving residents on the Treasure Coast in Florida. She believes living in a healthy home is essential to human health and well-being.

Cassy has an extensive blog and is a regular contributing writer for my publications, Wellness Real Estate Magazine™ and HealthyHOME™ Magazine. Learn more at www.wellnessbydezign.com

ASHLEY ROSE GONZALEZ

Let me introduce you to Ashley Rose, a remarkable real estate agent who embodies a passion for wellness in every aspect of her work. As a Green Realtor with One Sotheby's International Realty and Realty Sage, Ashley Rose is more than just a real estate professional—she's a Biophilic/Feng Shui Interior Designer. Ashley seamlessly integrates her spiritual practices into her clients' homes, infusing Reiki energy and the purifying essence of Sage and Palo Santo into every corner. Additionally, as a Culinary Alchemist Chef, she offers a personalized, home-cooked meal experience right in their new kitchens. Ashley's approach is all about crafting a unique and tailored experience for each client, catering to their individual needs. Her ultimate goal? To create a regenerative and sustainable process that not only leads clients to their dream homes but also gives back to the Earth. Welcome to Ashley Rose's world, where finding your Home Sweet Home is an enriching and holistic journey. You can find Ashley on Instagram her handle is @ashleyrose_sacredspaces

. . .

BRETT VREDEVOOGD

Brett Vredevoogd began his career in the sustainable residential industry as a builder in Bozeman, Montana, almost 20 years ago. He always knew he wanted to hone in on the sustainable side of the industry. Building with new technology and providing homes that are more energy-efficient was something that Brett is now passionate about. In 2013 Brett moved his family back to the midwest to focus on building a career in Real Estate. After finding NAR's GREEN Resource Council, he realized that he could infuse his passion for sustainability and green living into his real estate practice. Brett is now a NAR GREEN Designee and WellnessRE™PRO and serves residents of Grand Rapids, Michigan.

> "It has always been interesting to me that when selecting a new home, people rarely contemplate the cost of keeping it healthy and comfortable. It is by and large an afterthought that is often discovered within the first few months of homeownership, but it doesn't need to be that way." - Brett Vredevoogd

---

Connect with Brett at www.greenhomesgr.com

CHERI RILEY

Cheri is a Premier Sotheby's agent in Tampa Bay, Florida. She is a top-producing agent who actively networks with agents across the country. She works relentlessly on her client's behalf to help them achieve their real estate goals and make smart choices in the built environment. She is passionate about bringing the beauty of sustainable and environmentally friendly living to the luxury real estate market. Her community involvement and experience overseeing two billion dollars in sales during her real estate career serves her clients well. Learn more about Cheri at www.cheririley.com

CHRISTINA HATCH

Christina believes that home is more than just a location—it's a profound feeling. As a holistic REALTOR® in Pennsylvania, she is deeply passionate about providing her clients with a comprehensive and mindful approach to real estate. Christina not only assists families in finding homes but also guides them on transforming these spaces into healthy sanctuaries.

When it comes to sellers, Christina places a strong emphasis on reducing stress. She leverages her expertise and resources to ensure that the selling process is smooth and hassle-free. On her website, clients can access a wealth of information and resources related to healthy living, reflecting her commitment to their overall wellbeing. With Christina, the journey to finding or selling a home becomes not just a transaction, but a transformative experience focused on holistic living. You can find Christina at www.christinahatch.foxroach.com

CHRISTINE GREEN

Christine is a licensed REALTOR™ with a GREEN designation and WellnessRE™PRO serving the Greater Hartford, Connecticut area. She is passionate about community and healthy living and educates her clients not only on the home-buying journey but on the impact of choosing the right products for their home to make it a toxic-free, clean living environment. Connect with Christine on Facebook.

CHRISTOPHER MATOS-ROGERS

Christopher Matos-Rogers is an eco-agent in Atlanta, Georgia. His story began as a consumer simply looking for a home that would be suitable for his new electric vehicle. During his search, he realized every listing and buyer's agent knew little to nothing about this. His basic questions returned blank stares as agents struggled to find answers to specifics like where to locate the charging unit, how it was installed, and who locally could retrofit an existing home to be more energy efficient. He wondered if he was the only one asking these kinds of questions. Realizing there had to be more people like him, Christopher decided he would help this segment of the population that was incredibly underserved. He earned his real estate license shortly after that and has been a valuable guide for those searching for or selling energy-efficient homes for the past several years. Christopher walks the talk; he shares his energy upgrades with his audience, has been quick to help, and is involved in his local REALTOR® association. He has also participated in the National Association of REALTORS® conferences as a GREEN panelist. Recently, he won the Evergreen award given to exceptional agents by the NAR GREEN in 2021. Connect with Christopher on LinkedIN.

CINDY RODRIGUEZ

Cindy Rodriguez is Luxury Marketing Certified, New Home Buyer Certified, Green Accredited Professional with Sustainable Furnishings Council, a Certified Health Coach, NAR GREEN Designee and WellnessRE™PRO. She's a licensed Florida REALTOR®, and through her business, The Healthy Home Concierge, she serves residential design professionals, (such as Interior Designers, Architects, Builders, and other agents) by bringing wellness and sustainability components to their design projects, adding more dimension and value to their services. Learn more at www.thehealthyhomeconcierge.com

DANIEL HASON

Daniel Hason is a farmer turned regenerative real estate agent in upstate New York. Daniel grew up in NYC and moved upstate to get back in touch with nature and enjoy a more rural lifestyle. He was attracted to the local food movement and worked as a farmer for a few years before becoming a licensed REALTOR®. Like a magnet, he is attracting like-minded clients, by highlighting the importance of supporting local regenerative farmers in his conversations and marketing. Daniel continues to find the intersection of environmentalism and regenerative thinking in his real estate practice. Connect with Daniel at https://chooselatitude.com/danielhason

> Sidenote: If you want to learn more about regenerative farming, I suggest you watch the movie Kiss The Ground; it's available on Netflix and online.

EL LARSON

El Larson is a Feng Shui specialist, WELL AP, Fitwel Ambassador, REALTOR©, NAR GREEN Designee, and WellnessRE™ PRO serving residents in Pasadena, California. She works with spaces of all types to help clients find or create a home that supports their well-being. Blending evidence-based design strategies with ancient practices, our services include real estate sales, healthy building consulting, feng shui, and biophilic design. Connect with El at www.heare.agency.

HEATHER SCHMIDT

Heather Schmidt is a holistic REALTOR® and WellnessRE™PRO of the Holistic Real Estate Group in Plainfield, Illinois. She guides her clients through a positive real estate experience, empowering them to make decisions with their minds while leading with their hearts, and staying in alignment with their values. Her experience with Raike allows her to understand the energy in homes, and she performs space clearings so difficult properties can sell. Connect with Heather on Facebook.

GAIL CORCORAN

Gail Corcoran will passionately tell you that, in only a few short years, it's all going to come down to living "green"! She believes that real estate provides an excellent place for us to review our everyday choices of existence...whether one hopes to build a brand new home, seeks to purchase an existing one, or has no intention whatsoever of moving in the immediate future. As a NAR Green Designee, WellnessRE™PRO certified negotiation expert, and EPro, she uses those skills to help her clients become more aware of the possibilities of creating a home environment that is healthier and green. Connect with Gail at www.gailcorcoran.realtor

. . .

KARLA MULLINS

With a holistic healthcare degree with an emphasis on whole foods and herbalism, and being a Feng Shui Certified Consultant, Life Coach, and WellnessRE™PRO, Karla Mullins has a lot to offer residents in Wenatchee Washington. Whether it's buying, selling, or improving your existing home, her mission is to help lay the foundation, so they can be more resilient and handle the stresses of life, by being their holistic REALTOR®, Feng Shui consultant, and wellness friend. Connect with Karla at www.karlamullins.com

KATERINA SAYLES

Katerina Sayles is the founder of NW Green Living in Seattle, Washington. As a LEED Green Associate, NAR Green Designee, and WellnessRE™PRO, Katerina is dedicated to meeting each client's needs in buying or selling real estate, one that specializes in a new generation of green & healthy properties, which integrates wellness design and strategies to support a healthier home and work environment for years to come. Connect with Katerina at www.NWGreenliving.com & www.katerinasaylesrealtor.com

KRISTY WOODFORD

Kristy Woodford is a WellnessRE™PRO serving residents in Olympia, Washington. She specializes in a holistic approach to real estate with greater health, less stress, and more success in the process. Connect with Kristy at www.holistichomegroup.com

LAUREN CHIANG

Lauren, a Hawaii-based real estate agent, specializes in Wellness Travel—a fascinating niche in the real estate market. An intriguing trend is emerging in other countries like the Philippines, where luxury resorts are being developed to offer not only lavish accommodations but also top-tier medical treatments and care. These resorts also provide opportunities for property ownership, creating a unique fusion of luxury living and healthcare services.

Connect with Lauren on LinkedIN and check out this amazing property she represents: www.thefarmatsanbenito.com

NINA PATEL

Nina Patel is an agent in Houston, TX. She uses her knowledge and experience as a certified yoga instructor to include more mindfulness and intention in her real estate business. Calling herself the mindful agent may get some unusual looks, but agents who know her know that she's the real deal. She has mastered the art of meeting with clients and knowing which home is right for them. She will attribute it to her listening skills and asking the right questions, but she allows her intuition to help guide her to the right home for her clients. Considering that she's been a top producer for ReMAX fine properties for several years running, she must be doing something right! Connect with Nina on LinkedIN

SANDRA BARCKHOLTZ

Sandra earned her Green Designation to further assist clients with their desire for homes in a healthy, toxin-free environment. She is also a member of The Institute for Luxury Home Marketing and a Certified Luxury Home Marketing Specialist. As an avid equestrian, she specializes in horse properties and matching clients to properties that match their lifestyles. Connect with Sandra at www.sandrabarckholtz.evrealestate.com

SHELLEY GRUEN

Shelly Gruen is a REALTOR® serving residents in Palm Beach and Broward County, Florida. She's a NAR GREEN Designee and WellnessRF™PRO. Shelley is a people-focused strategic thinker who helps clients clarify their home goals and guide them through successful and healthy transactions. Connect with Shelley at www.shelleysellsflorida.com

. . .

TAMMI HOERNER

Tammi is a REALTOR® located in Parker Colorado. She aims to be the connector in her community and to offer next level service going above and beyond for her clients. As a WellnessRE PRO, she is infusing her passion for healthy living into her business and guiding buyers and sellers with integrity and honesty in residential, land, and luxury. Learn more about Tammi at www.sweethomescolorado.net

TERRY BROWN

Terry Brown helps home buyers and sellers in Atlanta, Georgia. She works with first-time home buyers and she's a senior home specialist, certified health coach, and WellnessRE™PRO. As an agent, Terry listens to the needs and preferences of each of her clients and uses her experience as a health coach and training in interior design to help her clients learn how their homes can be beautiful, green, and healthy. Connect with Terry on Facebook

TORI MCGEE

Tori McGee became a real estate agent when she realized the need for agents who understood the components of a healthy home after her own home search left her feeling like she knew much more about this than her local agents. Because she is a certified Building Biology Advocate, a

SHEILA ALSTON

Holistic REALTOR®, the Founder of Non-Toxic Georgia, a NAR Green Designee, and WellnessRE™PRO, Tori is able to connect residents in Atlanta with non-toxic companies, radon & mold testing, and clean water & air. Even those who have 5-G concerns can come to Tori for assistance, and she helps them learn how to create a more non-toxic living environment. Connect with Tori at www.atlantaholisticrealtor.com

---

Every day I meet new business owners helping people create healthier living spaces. It's so inspiring to me to see their positive energy and enthusiasm for what they do. I hope these few examples inspire you to think more about what you want your brand to represent. I also hope it gives you the courage to think outside the box and bring some of yourself, your values, and what is important to you to your brand identity. Check our overgrowing list of wellness experts here: https://www.healthy-home.pro/expertdirectory

I've noticed a widespread trend in our industry where agents proudly proclaim to be '#1'—whether on a team or with a broker. This self-promotion has saturated the market, creating a sea of noise where no individual voice stands out. It's easy to wonder, do clients truly care about how great *YOU* are? In my experience, I've found that when the focus shifts from our accomplishments to our clients, when we treat them as if *THEY* are truly #1, that's when we become the guiding force they're seeking. It's not just about selling homes; it's about crafting an experience that resonates on a personal level. ***So now, it's your time to shine.***

CHAPTER 6
WELLNESS LIFESTYLE COMMUNITIES

"If you want to change the world, you should start in your own backyard." - Serenbe founder, Steve Nygren

In the ever-evolving landscape of real estate development, the growth and positive change we're witnessing are nothing short of remarkable. Wellness lifestyle communities have emerged as beacons of this transformation, offering individuals and families a chance to live in harmony with nature and prioritize their well-being. In my exploration, I've discovered five distinct types of these communities as explained in Chapter 1:

- **Agrihoods**, where farm-to-table living takes center stage, fostering not just a connection to the land but also vibrant community interactions.
- **Naturehoods**, which seamlessly blend urban amenities with natural beauty, catering to the rising demand for Surban living—a trend that is set to shape the next decade.
- **Leisurehoods**, reminiscent of luxurious resort living, have become permanent havens where residents indulge in spa-like experiences every day.
- **Urban Wellness Communities** redefine city living, integrating healthy dining options, diverse workout facilities, and alternative medical treatments within the energetic pulse of urban spaces.
- Finally, the rise of **Minimalist or Tiny Living** is empowering individuals to embrace a 'less is more' philosophy, offering the freedom to explore the world unburdened by excess possessions.

These communities signify a paradigm shift, not just in the concept of home, but in the way we live, fostering connections, simplicity, and well-being at every turn.

The very first agrihood is located just outside Atlanta, Georgia, called Serenbe. The founder, Steve Nygren, and his wife Marie bought a country home for their children to be able to run, play and connect with nature. These weekend trips transformed their family, and soon they moved there full time. After a few years of living there, they became aware of the urban sprawl threatening to take over their beloved rural land. In an effort to protect their land from being overdeveloped and turned into strip malls, the Nygren's spearheaded a brand new kind of community, one where all residents thrive because their well-being was at the heart of the planning and design.

> "Serenbe is an award-winning biophilic community that connects people to nature and each other. The first house at Serenbe was built in 2004 and today the community is home to over 650 residents. Serenbe has won numerous awards including the Urban Land Institute Inaugural Sustainability Award, and the Atlanta Regional Commission "Development of Excellence" EarthCraft named Serenbe the "Development of the Year."[13]

I've also had the pleasure of interviewing Garnie Nygren, the daughter of Steve and Marie Nygren. She has told me that Serenbe has grown into a walkable mini-village where residents thrive because they love living there. It's like going back in time to an idyllic community where all the neighbors are friends and kids play and use their imaginations outdoors.

Many other forward-thinking developers have visited Serenbe and used it as a model to strive for.

Here is a small list of wellness lifestyle communities that I am aware of. Many of them I have featured in my digital magazines, WellnessRE™, HealthyHOME™ and Wellness@HOME™, where we explore wellness in real estate and help readers create a healthier home environment.

Arizona

- Agritopia Gilbert, Arizona

California

- Cannery Davis, California
- Esencia Mission Viejo, California
- Fanita Ranch Santee, California
- Fox Point Farms Encinitas, California
- I.D.E.A District San Diego, California
- Mighty Buildings Rancho Mirage, California
- Miralon Palm Springs, California

- North River Farms Oceanside, California
- Rancho Mission Viejo Mission Viejo, California
- Walden Monterey Monterey, California
- Win6 Village Santa Clara, California

COLORADO

- Agriburbia Brighton, Colorado
- Aria Denver, Colorado
- Baseline Broomfield, Colorado
- Bucking Horse Fort Collins, Colorado
- Dry Creek Ranch Eagle, Idaho
- Fox Hill Franktown, Colorado
- Mariposa Denver, Colorado
- S'Park Boulder, Colorado
- Sterling Ranch Denver, Colorado

FLORIDA

- Angeline Tampa, Florida
- Arden Palm Beach County, Florida
- Lake Nona Orlando, Florida
- Pine Dove Farm Tallahassee, Florida
- Shearwater St. Augustine, Florida
- The Grow Orlando, Florida
- The Packing District Orlando, Florida

GEORGIA

- Eco Cottages Atlanta, Georgia
- Serenbe Atlanta, Georgia

HAWAII

- Hokonui Maui, Hawaii
- Kukuiula Kuai, Hawaii
- Kuwililani Big Island Hawaii

IDAHO

- Hidden Springs Boise, Idaho

ILLINOIS

- Prairie Crossing Grayslake, Illinois
- Serosun Farms Hampshire, Illinois

INDIANA

- Tyron Farm Michigan City, Indiana

IOWA

- Middlebrook Farm Des Moines, Iowa

MINNESOTA

- White Oaks Savanna Stillwater Minnesota

MISSOURI

- Farmers Park Springfield, Missouri

NEW JERSEY

- Pendry Natirar Peapack, New Jersey
- Urby Harrison, New Jersey

NEW MEXICO

- Mesilla Vineyard La Cruces, New Mexico

NORTH CAROLINA

- Balsam Mountain Preserve Sylva, North Carolina
- Olivette Ashville, North Carolina
- River Bluffs Wilmington, North Carolina
- Urban Farm at Aldersgate - Charlotte, North Carolina

NEBRASKA

- Gardenview Lincoln Nebraska

OKLAHOMA

- Carlton Landing Lake Eufaula, Oklahoma

OHIO

- Aberlin Springs Morrow, Ohio

OREGON

- Pringle Creek Salem, Oregon

PENNSYLVANIA

- Amblebrook Gettysburg, Pennsylvania

SOUTH CAROLINA

- The Cliffs at Mountain Park Marietta, South Carolina

TENNESSEE

- Berry Farms Franklin, Tennessee
- Harvest Point Spring Hill, Tennessee
- Springbrook Farm Alcoa, Tennessee

TEXAS

- Harvest Argyle, Texas
- Harvest Green Richmond, Texas
- Millican Reserve College Station, Texas
- Orchard Ridge Liberty Hill, Texas
- Village Farm Austin, Texas
- Whisper Valley Austin, Texas

VERMONT

- Cobb Hill Co-Housing Harland, Vermont
- South Village South Burlington, Vermont

VIRGINIA

- Bundoran Farm North Garden, Virginia
- Chickahominy Falls Hanover County, Virginia
- Willowsford Loudoun County, Virginia

WASHINGTON

- The Grow Community Bainbridge Island, Washington

- Stackhouse Apartments Seattle, Washington

WISCONSIN

- Agape Mukwanago, Wisconsin

OTHER WELLNESS LIFESTYLE COMMUNITIES

- NW Bicester England
- One Planet Living, BedZed London, England
- TAOMexico Mexico

If you know of any others, please let us know so we can update our list!

hello@healthyhomemedia.com

NEXT STEPS

I hope this book has sparked a fire within you, inspiring you not only to think differently but to act differently in your real estate endeavors. It's more than just a shift in strategy; it's a transformational change that will not only make a positive impact in the lives of others but also significantly elevate your business. I understand the challenges you face - the inconsistent leads, the lack of security - and I want you to recognize that the power to change your circumstances lies within your grasp.

With the strategies in this book, you now have new avenues to create a significant positive impact in the world through your work as a real estate agent. Knowing that there are professionals like you, driven by a genuine desire to make a difference, warms my heart. It's a testament to the fact that there are agents and industry experts out there who prioritize meaningful connections over mere transactions. Your willingness to help others and contribute positively to the world is what sets you apart, and I have full confidence that your journey ahead will be both fulfilling and impactful.

When you prioritize people and give wholeheartedly, not only does your business thrive, but you also close more deals. Clients are yearning for genuine connections, and when they see your authenticity shining through, they're not just clients anymore; they become loyal advocates and cheerleaders. Take this opportunity today to have authentic conversations, expand your reach, and build an unmistakable brand. Remember, if you don't take action, nothing will change. The path to a more secure, fulfilling career is right here before you. Seize it. What do you have to lose? Embrace this moment, embrace the change, and watch your real estate journey soar to unprecedented heights. Your empowered future starts with your choice to act today.

Here's to a future of meaningful interactions and transformative experiences in the realm of real estate!

If you'd like access to some of the free resources I've created for you that I mentioned earlier in this book: the conversation starters, the 30 social media ideas and the healthy home checklist, simply head to https://www.healthyhomemedia.com/wellnessrebook to grab those for yourself. I'll include the PDF download and also the Canva template link to the checklist so you can customize it without having to start from scratch.

NEXT STEPS

I so appreciate you, and I'd like to ask you a small favor. If you enjoyed this book and found anything in it to be helpful, please write a review. You can do this by downloading the free resources at www.healthyhomemedia.com/wellnessrebook there will be a link there or you can go to Amazon and search wellness real estate. Either way would help other agents like you find the book.

I'd love to know what you enjoyed most about the book! Not only will this let others know what's inside the book so that they can make an informed decision as to whether it's a good book for them, but I do read every single one of them! I'm doing my best to make sure that everything I'm working on in some way provides value to others, so I'd love your honest feedback to know what you enjoyed most about this book! I know I'm not perfect, but I am taking small steps every day to move closer to the goals I want to achieve, and I hope that I can be an inspiration to you too. You are amazing, you are strong, you are resilient, and you are the connector in your community! Your future clients need your help! The small daily actions you take are the building blocks of significant change. By consistently prioritizing people and authenticity, you're not just transforming your business; you're making a lasting impact on the world. Your dedication and genuine approach will ripple out, inspiring others and creating a wave of positive change. Keep believing in the power of your actions, for it's through these daily choices that you shape a better future, not only for your clients but for the world at large.

Together, we are making this world a healthier place, one home at a time.

Afterward

As of late 2022, I am no longer an active agent, instead, I'm focusing on helping agents just like you grow their businesses. In 2020 I started a digital magazine called the Wellness Real Estate Magazine™ or WellnessRE™ so I could share news and healthy home tips with my audience. It was a lot of work to create and so I thought I'd share it with other agents. Since then, my membership has grown and I now have a tribe of wellness agents around the country who use my tools to create more conversations with people about their businesses and differentiate their brands. Through this journey, I have learned that even though I was making more money as an active agent, my true passion is to help struggling agents and agents who want to reach more people. It has brought me so much joy to learn how my marketing tools are helping them win more clients and educate more people. Like this story about Terry Brown from Atlanta, GA. She recently snagged **25 new leads in one day** at a local jazz festival – just by sharing her custom-branded issues of WellnessRE Magazine. People didn't just sign up for her email list; they eagerly embraced their journey toward healthier homes. Talk about game-changer!

But don't just take my word for it:

"WellnessRE™ Magazine has helped me grow my brand significantly! I have a whole group of followers that now look forward to reading new issues every month. They actually thank me for sharing tips with them on creating a healthier home." - Tori McGee, Atlanta GA Holistic REALTOR®

INCREDIBLE MARKETING TOOLS

"Leading with this magazine has opened up so many more conversations and continues to help me generate new followers everywhere I go! I now have marketing materials I'm proud to share at listing presentations, open houses, and even with my entire partner network!

My custom-branded magazine has helped me secure several listings, including a new one for a $6M home just this week!!!"

C. Craig San Diego, CA REALTOR®

Healthy Home Media is a great resource for building my brand AND delivering valuable content to my clients

NEXT STEPS

H. Schmidt, Plainfield, IL REALTOR®

If you would like access to done-for-you marketing tools specifically for real estate agents and healthy home professionals that help them engage and connect with more people about your business, then head over to: www.healthyhomemedia.com

Use this coupon code, **WRBOOK25,** for $25 off membership to WellnessRE™PRO or HealthyHOME™PRO.

We want to connect you with other forward-thinking industry professionals, to be a part of our tribe, to collaborate, connect, and to refer! I invite you to join our free Facebook group at www.facebook.com/groups/wellnessre

REFERENCES

1. Global Wellness Institute. (2021, September 27). *Wellness Real Estate Market Nearly Doubles from 2017-2020–Jumping from $148 to $275 Billion*. https://globalwellnessinstitute.org/press-room/press-releases/wellness-real-estate-market/
2. Technavio, (2023, June 26), Wellness real estate market size is to grow by USD 575.9 billion from 2022 to 2027; increasing demand for regenerative living to be an emerging trend. https://www.prnewswire.com/news-releases/wellness-real-estate-market-size-is-to-grow-by-usd-575-9-billion-from-2022-to-2027-increasing-demand-for-regenerative-living-to-be-an-emerging-trend---technavio-301862675.html
3. Global Wellness Institute. (2021, September 27). *Wellness Real Estate Market Nearly Doubles from 2017-2020–Jumping from $148 to $275 Billion*. https://globalwellnessinstitute.org/press-room/press-releases/wellness-real-estate-market/
4. *"Surban" Areas – Bringing Suburban and Urban Together*. (2018, June 12). reonomy.com. https://www.reonomy.com/blog/post/surban-areas-bringing-suburban-and-urban-areas-together
5. Statista. (n.d.). *Statista - The Statistics Portal*. https://www.statista.com/markets/460/topic/599/residential-real-estate/
6. *Multigenerational Living: New Take on an Old Tradition*. (2020, April 17). www.nar.realtor. https://www.nar.realtor/magazine/real-estate-news/home-and-design/multigenerational-living-new-take-on-an-old-tradition

REFERENCES

7. *Quick Real Estate Statistics*. (2015, June 23). www.nar.realtor. https://www.nar.realtor/research-and-statistics/quick-real-estate-statistics
8. health enews Staff. (2014, August 29). *How germ-free is your kitchen*. Health Enews. https://www.ahchealthenews.com/2014/08/29/how-germ-free-is-your-kitchen/
9. health enews Staff. (2015, February 19). *5 tips for a germ-free home*. Health Enews. https://www.ahchealthenews.com/2013/11/14/3-tips-to-help-keep-your-home-germ-free/
10. Weber, E. L. A. V. (2008, June 17). *How Dirty Are Your Shoes?* ABC News. https://abcnews.go.com/GMA/Consumer/story?id=5177409
11. Shahyd, K. (n.d.). *Residential Energy Efficiency is Largest Source of CO2 Reduction Potential*. NRDC. https://www.nrdc.org/experts/khalil-shahyd/residential-energy-efficiency-largest-source-co2-reduction-potential
12. Solar Energy Industries Organization. (2017, June 8). Solar Spotlight California. *Www.Seia.Org*. https://www.seia.org/sites/default/files/2017%20Q1%20CA.pdf
13. *Comparison of Green Building Standards*. (2022, May 12). US EPA. https://www.epa.gov/smartgrowth/comparison-green-building-standards
14. *Serenbe*. (n.d.). https://www.serenbe.com/
15. *79% of people say wellness is important*, (2021, April 18), McKinsey.com https://www.mckinsey.com/industries/consumer-packaged-goods/our-insights/feeling-good-the-future-of-the-1-5-trillion-wellness-market

Bringhurst, Robert. *The Elements of Typographic Style*. Version 3.2. Point Roberts: Hartley & Marks, 2004.

REFERENCES

The Chicago Manual of Style. 17th ed. The University of Chicago Press Editorial Staff. Chicago: The University of Chicago Press, 2017. https://www.chicagomanualofstyle.org/.

Vellum Tutorial. Updated regularly. Oakland and Seattle: 180g. https://help.vellum.pub/tutorial/.

Made in the USA
Columbia, SC
25 October 2023